T0274159

OUR FOUNDERS' WARNING

The Age of Reason

Meets the Age of Trump

STROBE TALBOTT

BROOKINGS INSTITUTION PRESS
Washington, D.C.

Copyright © 2020
THE BROOKINGS INSTITUTION
1775 Massachusetts Avenue, N.W.
Washington, D.C. 20036
www.brookings.edu

The Brookings Institution is a private nonprofit organization devoted to research, education, and publication on important issues of domestic and foreign policy. Its principal purpose is to bring the highest quality independent
research and analysis to bear on current and emerging policy problems. Inter-
pretations or conclusions in Brookings publications should be understood to
be solely those of the authors.

Library of Congress Control Number: 2020938100
ISBN 9780815738237 (hc)
ISBN 9780815738244 (ebook)

9 8 7 6 5 4 3 2 1

Typeset in Cheltenham

Composition by Elliott Beard

To Barbara and our families

O! Ye unborn Inhabitants of America! Should this Page escape its destined Conflagration at the Year's End, and these Alphabetical Letters remain legible, — when your Eyes behold the Sun after he has rolled the Seasons round for two or three centuries more, you will know that in Anno Domini 1758, we dreamed of your times.

—Nathaniel Ames, publisher of the first
annual American almanac

————

Posterity! You will never know how much it cost the present generation to preserve your freedom! I hope you will make a good use of it. If you do not, I shall repent in Heaven that I ever took half the pains to preserve it.

—John Adams, in a letter to Abigail, April 26, 1777

————

However [political parties] may now and then answer popular ends, they are likely in the course of time and things, to become potent engines, by which cunning, ambitious, and unprincipled men will be enabled to subvert the power of the people and to usurp for themselves the reins of government, destroying afterwards the very engines which have lifted them to unjust dominion.

—George Washington's Farewell Address

Contents

Preface

During the first months of the coronavirus pandemic, while I was finishing this book, my wife and I were self-quarantined in a hamlet far out on Long Island, New York. I would take a noon break to tune into Governor Andrew Cuomo's daily update on the pandemic that was devastating the state more than any other. Following his remarks and before taking questions from the press, he would recite a variation of a mantra: "New Yorkers are tough, smart, united, disciplined, and loving." The refrain was not just a grace note; his congratulations were a reminder to his fellow citizens of their responsibility for a working democracy.

Toward the end of each day, I would put away the manuscript and watch Donald Trump's briefing from the White House. His objective, as always, was to congratulate himself. His toughness is that of a bully. He made sure that the world thought he was a genius who could outsmart the experts. Divide and conquer has been his grand strategy. Discipline meant absolute fealty to his caprices. His self-love is so cavernous that there is little space for anyone or anything else. He spews hatred at those who oppose him or get in the way of his personal vanities and goals.

These deformations were also on gruesome display when a Minneapolis police officer choked to death George Floyd, a Black man, in broad daylight. Trump urged an indiscriminate crackdown against mostly peaceful protests and threatened to put the country under martial law.

There was an eerie overlap between a global pestilence and another case of lethal police brutality against a Black person. As American fatalities rose beyond a hundred thousand, many of the victims died because, like George Floyd, they couldn't breathe. His last cries echoed the anguish of his race.

———

In Trump's 2017 inaugural address, he accused his precursors of "this American carnage," and he vowed he would "end it right here and now," whatever it was. That gratuitous slur will haunt him now that he has stoked two real tragedies.

Before the virus sneaked into coastal America and a chance recording of George Floyd's death went viral from the heartland to the world, Trump had already grievously damaged our polity, society, and nation's reputation in the world.

The body politic of our country has been panting through

four years of Trump's reign. Multiple sectors in the U.S. electorate have a vital stake in defeating Trump. They will be looking
to the future, but they will also be surrogates for the founders of
the American republic. Those long-dead men did their best to
ensure a set of noble principles and durable institutions for their
successors to steward.

They were worried. Their letters and speeches were often
flares shot over the horizon in the hope that posterity would heed
their warnings.

In these pages, I have tried to refresh the memory of what our
founders did, as well as why and how they did it. I hope, within
that historical context, Trumpism can be seen more clearly as a
concerted effort to undo the foundation of our government.

––––––––

I am a student of history, not a historian. My first and longest
profession was journalism. The term makes explicit that the
news is new, ripe for the day. After more than two decades at
Time magazine, I was recruited into government in the 1990s,
then think-tankery. Both pursuits dealt with the here-and-now.
My previous experience as a reporter helped me uncover the nub
of a coherent, accurate story and explain why it mattered.

There is another advantage for a newshound retelling the
story of America's origin: the protagonists were ahead of their
time. They were not just waiting to see what the future would
bring—they were *planning* for it, *building* it.

Reading primary sources has often felt as though I was interviewing the founders. Their personalities are still vivid, their assertions articulate, their debates vigorous.

Still, I have leaned heavily on patient historians who have explored for decades the goals, attitudes, values, and decisions that brought forth a country, an ideology, and a movement abroad. Scholars explaining the eighteenth century avoid what they call presentism. For most of us, the past is a foreign country. Those who lived there had different mores, fears, prejudices, and hopes. Even some evocative English words have different meanings now.

My present-day tutors have aided my understanding of those distant but eloquent voices. Afterall, the founders' exploits, innovations, dreams, fears—and warnings—are not just woven into the national memory; they are part of the backstory of our current predicament.

————

Americans of my generation are, for the second time, living through a constitutional crisis created by a rogue president. In 1974, I was a rookie in *Time*'s Washington bureau, assigned to a burgeoning investigation into Richard Nixon's cover-up of a burglary at the Democratic National Committee headquarters in the Watergate Hotel. The American people and their representatives dealt with the challenge successfully. When the two parties recognized that a crime was initiated in the Oval Office, Nixon's presidency self-destructed.

The capital returned to its normal level of modulated frenzy, and the nation and the world gave a deep sigh. Words like *plumbers* and *unindicted co-conspirator* had become part of the popular vocabulary. So had idioms of the day: "What did the President know and when did he know it?" and "a cancer on the presidency."

After Gerald Ford took the oath of office, he said, "My fellow Americans, our long national nightmare is over. Our Constitution works. Our great Republic is a government of laws and not of men. Here the people rule." His words had a soothing effect on the nation.

Not only did the two parties come together in the Congress, they also had done historical homework. The Committee on the Judiciary in the House of Representatives commissioned a task-force of academic experts to compile a crash course on scandals and controversies under all previous presidents. The professors worked intensely under the chairmanship of C. Vann Woodward, a renowned historian at Yale. In the introduction of the published report, he elevated the founder-presidents to a class by themselves. They were, he wrote, "[m]en of enormous prestige and formidable integrity, [who] held rigid standards of conduct and scrupulous regard for the Constitution. They or their friends had written it."[1]

By the time the Woodward report was published, America was preparing to celebrate the bicentennial of the Declaration of Independence. Readers wanted elevating fare that matched the mood. They turned to a bumper crop of books about that early drama and its heroes. Inspiring biographies kept coming.

Two decades later, the Obama phenomenon—the man and the diverse citizenry that elected him—kept optimism and progress alive. The system worked, or so it seemed.

Then, forty-two years after the bicentennial, came the Trump insurgency. A 2018 *New Yorker* article lifted the Woodward book from obscurity. The author, Jill Lepore, contacted several contributors. Among them was William McFeely, an emeritus professor at the University of Georgia. She asked him to compare Nixon's and Trump's miscreancies: "I think Nixon was pretty bad, but I think that even he had a respect for the Constitution, and for a constitutional sense of the value of the presidency. Trump trounces on those."[2]

McFeely died at 89 in Sleepy Hollow, New York, on December 11, 2019, a week before the House of Representatives impeached Trump, knowing that the Senate would acquit him. More than that, the majority turned the process into a farcical prosecution of the Constitution. Trump and his allies played the outcome as a vindication of his malignant persona and agenda.

Then the world seemed to shift on its axis, throwing Trump on the defensive. But at the time of this writing, I wouldn't say that the system is working.

SPRINGS, NEW YORK
June 24, 2020

OUR FOUNDERS' WARNING

1

The Man Who Would Be King

Age: A portion of human history distinguished
by certain characters real and mythical

—*Oxford English Dictionary*

Early in Donald Trump's run for the world's most powerful office, an unusual dispute swirled around the word *normal*. To his supporters, *normal* meant bland, phony, corrupt. "He's the grizzly bear in the room," declared Newt Gingrich gleefully. "He's not normal"—meaning he's exciting, authentic, the real deal.[1] From the opposing camp, Hillary Clinton, warning against extremist political behavior, vowed, "My campaign is not going to let Donald Trump try to normalize himself."[2]

Trump knew exactly what he was doing. He was bending the process to his will, separating himself from the other aspirants for the nomination, cowing the Republican establishment, breaking rules to his advantage, and beating the odds.

The 2016 election was the most surprising upset since Truman beat Dewey in 1948. Only a few Cassandras had taken Trump seriously. After the New Hampshire primary, the first of a long stretch of the unlikely insurgent's victories, Eliot Cohen, a professor of political science and veteran of past Republican administrations, published an essay titled "The Age of Trump."[3]

"How on earth," Cohen begins, "did this happen?" Conservative analysts, he notes, have offered some explanations—economic stagnation, "shifting class structure," "existential anxiety about . . . a robot-driven economy," and "liberal overreach in social policy." They have also acknowledged "Trump's formidable political skills, including a visceral instinct for detecting and exploiting vulnerability that has been the hallmark of many an authoritarian ruler. These insights are all to the point, but they do not capture one key element. Moral rot. Politicians have, since ancient Greece, lied, pandered, and whored. They have taken bribes, connived, and perjured themselves. But in recent times—in the United States, at any rate—there has never been any politician quite as openly debased and debauched as Donald Trump."[4]

After Trump laid waste to the field of competitors and clinched the Republican nomination, Jonathan Freedland, a British journalist writing in *The Guardian*, positioned the Trump juggernaut within a global contagion of populism and nativism: "This rage at the system—the fuming insistence that democracy is failing to deliver for the people it's meant to serve, that the system that bears its name is no longer truly democratic— powers not just Trump but many of the populist movements now making waves around the world."[5]

Freedland's headline, "Welcome to the Age of Trump," echoed Cohen's. By election day, the expression had long since gone viral.[6] For decades the flamboyant real estate mogul had emblazoned his name on tall buildings around the world. Now his brand personalized a global era. Classifying distinct periods of the American saga with presidents' names has been a custom among biographers to honor presidents who were in their graves.[7] Trump, nearly a year before he was inaugurated, had the pleasure of seeing his name celebrated for years and possibly decades to come.

Never mind that the phrase Age of Trump was meant to imply dark and dangerous times ahead. His detractors who coined it would have to live with his apotheosis and their gloom.

Trump denigrates the intellectual elites while proclaiming that he is one of them—only smarter. He has often bragged of being "a sort of genius." At a campaign rally, Trump rhapsodized on his brilliant career by declaring, "I went to an Ivy League school! I'm very highly educated. I know words. I have the best words."[8]

———

For nearly half his life, Trump had flirted with mounting a crusade to the White House. The Great Recession at the end of the first decade of the twenty-first century presented him with a long shot. Radical conservatives blamed the troubled economy on a bloated and corrupt American government that had neglected a largely white middle class while coddling other ethnic communities. The result was a movement that skewed the Republican Party's center of gravity toward the far right, energizing populists and nativists. The leaders dubbed their crusade the Tea Party, a travesty in itself. The original Tea Party, in 1773, was a seminal event uniting what would be an independent American republic; its sham namesake incited the opposite.[9]

It took two presidential election cycles for the movement to gain control. In 2008 and 2012, the GOP nominated moderate, experienced, reputable candidates, John McCain and Mitt Romney, respectively. Yet Barack Obama—a new face but a candidate with venerable virtues—was able to defeat both challengers.

In 2016 Hillary Clinton's campaign sailed into a perfect storm while Trump had the wind at his back, aided by the most unlikely couple: the president of Russia (who knew exactly what he was doing) and the director of the Federal Bureau of Investigation (who apparently did not).

Much to the dismay of political veterans, Trump's instincts and tactics served him well. Conventional wisdom held that he was his own worst enemy. In fact, he was appealing to a critical mass of Americans who were frightened of the future, disillusioned with the present, nostalgic for the past, and disaffected with politics as usual. He gleefully broke rules of etiquette, separated himself from the other aspirants for the Republican nomination, and made it clear that he was going to remake the presidency in his own image: iconoclastic, boastful, self-reliant, pugnacious, and disruptive.

Trump was doubling down on a procedural paradox of American self-rule: a presidential election should be a dignified process, but in reality, it is politics as war by other means. The word *campaign* itself originated from the French for an army on the march in the seventeenth-century Wars of Religion. Modern times have added more martial jargon: attack ads, money bombs, battleground states, and—a new phrase and an ominous innovation—the weaponization of social media.

The ordeal of the political campaign has always left wounds on those citizens who voted for the loser. The winner has typically seen it in his own interest, as well as the nation's, to restore civic peace.

Not Trump. His presidency has been an escalation of his campaign. Armed with the powers of office, he has given no quarter to his fellow citizens and public officials who oppose him.

———

In the days and weeks that followed his election, Trump presented himself as a tough, cocky new CEO, bent on a hostile takeover.[10] He set his sights on his recent predecessors. And his attacks were personal. His animus toward Barack Obama was most obvious, but he also belittled George W. Bush, Bill Clinton, George H. W. Bush, and Jimmy Carter for their "failures" of domestic policy and diplomacy.[11]

Trump's habit of blanket disparagement goes further back than recent presidents. He spurned the role of the United States as master builder of the liberal international order left to him by twelve commanders in chief—six Republicans and six Democrats in the aftermath of World War II. In place of the American Century, Trump proclaimed a new stance and what he thought was a new catchphrase, America First.

At the Republican National Convention on July 21, 2016, Trump gave an interview to David Sanger and Maggie Haberman of the *New York Times*. When Sanger remarked that the go-it-alone policy sounded like Charles Lindbergh's America

First, Trump reacted as though he had never heard the phrase, then, on the spot, made it his own tagline. He seemed oblivious of the slogan's disrepute. "To me," Trump said, "America First is a brand-new modern term. I never related it to the past."[12] His ignorance of the motto's implication of anti-Semitism and appeasement of dictators, if genuine, clearly displayed Trump's combination of unabashed anti-historicism and ahistoricism.

The past, in Trump's view, is not prologue; it is either irrelevant or enemy territory. His iconic predecessors are, for him, rivals to outshine. Less than two years into the job, he asserted, "Nobody's ever done a better job than I'm doing as president."[13] That includes the founders. His jealousy of their mythic stature has been palpable in his instinct to disparage their legacies.

After a few months on the job, he let it be known to some of his golf partners that the White House was "a real dump."[14] He prefers to live in edifices that he owns and decorates at will, mostly with icons to himself. Instead, as president he must live with portraits of his stern-faced precursors, including at least six portraits of George Washington.

Trump is one of the noisiest of our presidents, but when it comes to the founders, he prefers to give them either the silent treatment or a gratuitous jab. One such incident occurred in a news conference in September 2018. The storm over his second Supreme Court nominee, Brett Kavanaugh, was at its peak.

While dismissing the reporters' sharp questions, Trump suggested that "if we brought George Washington here and we said we have George Washington [for the Court], the Democrats would vote against him; just so you understand, and he may have had a bad past. Who knows? He may have had some—I think—accusations made. Didn't he have a couple things in his past?"[15]

Misdirection and insinuation are among Trump's favorites ploys. In this case, he impugned the father of the nation, leaving the audience to puzzle over a rhetorical question that was both snide and murky. As the House of Representatives was preparing to impeach him in late 2019, Trump endorsed an encomium from Fox News's Lou Dobbs: "He's got me down as the greatest president in the history of our country, including George Washington and Abraham Lincoln."[16]

———

Trump has, however, approved of one previous president as a kindred spirit. The White House press corps has a tradition of asking a new president whom among his forebears he most admires. Stephen K. Bannon, Trump's Svengali at the time, convinced him to pick Andrew Jackson, the first antiestablishment president. Jackson campaigned as a champion of the common man and scourge of the corrupt autocracy.[17] When the forty-fifth president moved into the Oval Office, he brought with him a portrait of the seventh. Whether by chance or as Bannon's putdown of the liberal elites, Old Hickory had a special distinction of his own: he was the first president who was not one of the nation's founders.

Washington, John Adams, Thomas Jefferson, James Madison, and James Monroe were present at the creation of the United States. They were, in fact, among the primary creators. The sixth president, John Quincy Adams, had been at his father's side in Europe during the American Revolution. As a young man, he served as an envoy in his own right and as secretary of state before assuming the presidency.

Those six presidents, along with America's man for all seasons, Benjamin Franklin, are the protagonists of this book. Their joint legacy has been important in every stage of American history, but it is especially relevant in the current one. The founders put their individual and shared morals to work in the public arena, establishing the foundation of the freedom that is our national birthright.

———

The Founding Fathers of the American republic valued their own heritage as children of the European Enlightenment.[18] The movement emphasized the sovereignty of human beings, the capacity of individuals to reason, to seek knowledge, and to live by ethics based on honesty, tolerance, and empathy.

They forged these high-minded abstractions into tools for liberating their lands and liberalizing their governance. As a prominent American historian, Henry Steele Commager, put it, "The Old World imagined, invented, and formulated the Enlightenment; the New World—certainly the Anglo-American part of it—realized it and fulfilled it."[19]

The founders were men of affairs: landed farmers, lawyers, journalists, publishers, preachers, educators, scientists, physicians, and a retired soldier who had looked forward to a pastoral life on the banks of the Potomac River. When they renounced their allegiance to the British Crown, they designed an architecture of governance that the world had never seen.

The founders were not just lighting lamps: they were playing with fire, and they knew it. They were cautious optimists, not utopians. Nor were they saints or angels (most did not believe in such beings). Some of their failures cast dark clouds onto our day and as far as the eye can see into our own future. Race was the most intractable. Four centuries after the first slaves were forcibly brought to British America as chattel, their descendants have had to endure President Trump's dog whistles, watch him repress their right to vote, and hear him condone homegrown Nazis and other white supremacists.

The founders were not determinists, expecting that the arc of history, by itself, would bend toward equality, justice, liberty, and peace. Realization of those ideals required constant, judicious, and ethical human agency. Progress was fragile, susceptible to human weakness or malevolent strength.

———

The founders were acutely aware that their unique construct and valiant determination would be sorely tested. They knew that the customary instrument for maintaining order and exercising magisterial power was tyranny. Republics of the past had been fleeting anomalies, favored by idealists but not by most rulers who relied on the state's monopoly of violence to ensure their subjects' submission.

In the sweep of history, most of the leaders of tribes or nations or empires were ruled by the grizzly bear's instincts. Modern dictatorship is not a new normal: it is an ancient system making a comeback.[20]

John Adams was a fervent student of history and the founder most inclined to prophecy and mood swings. When gloomy, he feared that the republic would last only a few decades. He had trepidations that future Americans would not be up to the job— or, worse, that they might tack toward autocracy. He worried that a full-blooded demagogue could undermine the American experiment.[21]

———

A hoary adage defines journalism as the first draft of history. But those who have made history often have had their own drafts. First come the ideas; then comes the debates, often blood-spilled; then the words, first chiseled in stone, later handwritten on parchment; then, finally, the laws and institutions are created. Only when those rules and their means of enforcement have been established does the intended nation become a reality, with a government that begins to function.

The Declaration of Independence was a calculated act of hubris. The founders proceeded as if the United States of America were up and running. But the independence they sought was not yet theirs; it was left to their ragtag Continental Army to defeat the mightiest military in the world.

The signers were determined to wrest their homeland from Britain, but it would take seven bloody, crisis-ridden years to accomplish that goal. The self-evident principles they were fighting for might have been crushed. The founders were trying to do something almost unimaginable, something that would take a long, long time. Their bold, hazardous, and speculative venture needed fervent goals to match the bold chances they were taking.

The Declaration of Independence was meant to sing, to lift Americans' resolve and courage for what was to come. Moreover, the founders were taking personal responsibility for what they had already done and what they would do if they won the war. Had the revolution failed, they would have signed their death sentences. That gave their moral weight to the responsibilities they passed to their descendants.

The framers of the Constitution, however, had a different purpose. Whereas the Declaration of Independence was a secular psalm heralding timeless truths, the Constitution set perimeters for the inevitable, ongoing arguments about what those truths meant and how to turn them into laws.

The law of laws—the preeminent commandment—held that no one was above the law. The revolutionary generation maintained a crucial consistency through six administrations—spanning forty years, from 1789 to 1829—to solidify and extend that secular commandment into the twenty-first century. Now, under Trump, we can hear the tablets cracking.

2

Heaven, Earth, and the Mind

Know then thyself, presume not God to scan,
The proper study of mankind is Man.

—Alexander Pope, *An Essay on Man*

When Donald Trump accepted the Republican Party's presidential nomination in Cleveland, Ohio, in July 2016, his peroration brought down the house. It consisted of four one-syllable words, starting with his favorite: *"I* am your voice!" At a minimum, the punch line rang of hubris.

The founders would have gone further: they would have sensed the acrid odor of tyranny. In a republic, citizens must retain their voices and exercise their right to think for themselves. That principle was at the core of the founders' philosophy, and had been inculcated in many of them from their youth. They guarded it like a shield to the end of their days.

When Thomas Jefferson retired to his beloved Monticello overlooking Charlottesville, Virginia, he had a large collection of busts and paintings of his heroes in history. The English Enlightenment was well represented. High on the parlor wall, near the entrance, were three portraits: Francis Bacon, the father of empiricism; Isaac Newton, the father of modern science; and John Locke, the father of liberalism. Jefferson called them "my trinity of the three greatest men the world had ever produced."[1]

By dubbing these eminences a trinity, Jefferson might have

been taking a sly jab at religion in general and Christianity in particular. After all, he was one of the more forthright figures of the time and took a dim view of spiritual dogma.

Jefferson was a latter-day proponent of a radical movement at the end of the sixteenth century and early seventeenth whose adherents came to be called freethinkers. They trusted reason and logic, questioned conventional wisdom, and resisted conformity, especially religious doctrine.[2]

Over the decades, British philosophers, scientists, and political activists claimed mastery over their minds. By the eighteenth century, that ethos had permeated the intellectual climate of the British colonies in America. Thomas Paine, the English-born political theorist and pamphleteer for the Revolution, put the matter succinctly: "My own mind is my own church."[3]

The personalization of faith was crucial to the liberalization of politics—most consequentially, in what would become the United States of America. Many major founders were steeped in political and philosophical ancient Greece and Rome, but they also turned to their ancestral country and its reformers and scientists of the preceding century. A thirty-year-old John Adams asserted that the people "have a right, an indisputable, unalienable, indefeasible divine right to the most dreaded and envied kind of knowledge, I mean of the characters and conduct of their rulers."[4] He was making the case for the sovereignty of individual thought. Freethinking, which had begun on the fringes of the early Enlightenment, was transformed to be an essential element of an American credo.

———

Throughout previous periods, piety was often fused with patriotism, and ecclesiastical and secular orders reinforced each other. Rulers exercised their authority in the name of an all-powerful divine force that favored and protected their realms and thrones. The effect often galvanized and stabilized communities that became nations, enabling them to make great strides in science, philosophy, morality, civics, culture, education, and governance. But for millennia, the authoritarian symbiosis between princes and priests set limits on individual thought and teaching.

As the Enlightenment modernized and rationalized governance, it also constrained religion from influencing politics, laws, diplomacy—and war. The Protestant Reformation weakened Catholicism's claim to being the "universal" church of Christendom and limited the papacy's extensive temporal power. The Wars of Religion, starting in the sixteenth century, and the Thirty Years War, in the seventeenth, left millions dead.[5] Prompted by exhaustion, the combatants came together to end religious wars in Europe in a diplomatic marathon that led to the Peace of Westphalia between May and October 1648.

Intellectuals and scientists of seventeenth and eighteenth century Europe were more likely to question reigning orthodoxy if there was little risk of the ax, the gibbet, or the stake. They distributed their ideas while absorbing or disputing those of their peers.

The result was an international network of knowledge, often called the Republic of Letters. The unfettering of reason and imagination created a vast, kaleidoscopic configuration of science, philosophy, literature, music, architecture, theater, art, and medicine. At its center was the presumption that if answers to questions about the universe and humanity were to be found anywhere, they would only come from the mind of *Homo sapiens sapiens*, "man who knows that he knows." The human being is also *Homo curiosus*: before questioning, exploring, experimenting, and inventing, *Homo sapiens* yearns to know what is *not* known.

———

In searching for new knowledge and testing the old, these pioneering thinkers gave wide scope to inquisitiveness and skepticism.

One of them, Francis Bacon, was a devout Anglican who composed holy meditations and religious tracts, while his scientific work concentrated on phenomena that he could see, measure, and prove. Although Bacon believed in God's existence, he acknowledged that his rational methods could not prove it. He worshipped the almighty, all-wise creator of everything, but he did not look to the scriptures as he sought a way to explain the machinery of the universe.

Bacon's experiments worked inductively from a controlled collection of facts to general principles. Though devout, he emboldened some scientists and other freethinkers to question religious faith and put their trust in empiricism. Anthony Pagden, a professor of intellectual history, has written that those who made the transition to scientific and philosophic secularism were entering a "fatherless world."[6]

———

Enter Thomas Hobbes, growling. In his youth, Hobbes served Bacon as an amanuensis. While learning much from the renowned scientist, the two parted ways over Bacon's straddling of spiritual faith and rigorous logic. Hobbes was a staunch materialist, with the firm belief that matter, including gray matter, *matters*, and that conjuring incorporeal concepts, including God, was a waste of time.[7] Heaven and its celestial beings, he believed, were figments of imagination or, worse, superstitions foisted onto gullible minds.

Hobbes comes across in his writings as a philosophic curmudgeon of Enlightenment noir. He perceived "the life of man solitary, poor, nasty, brutish, and short" and his own birth the arrival of "the little worm."[8] Even moments of joy and mirth are viewed as schadenfreude or mere relief from misery: "Laughter is nothing else but a sudden glory arising from sudden conception of some eminency in ourselves, by comparison with the infirmities of others, or with our own formerly."[9]

In keeping with his grim, unforgiving view, Hobbes considered nature selfish, cruel, and ruthless competition. He was fond of the Latin proverb "Man is a wolf to man,"[10] and he translated Thucydides's *Peloponnesian War*, with its bleak implication that history itself is an epic of disasters.[11]

To fend off chaos and "the war of all against all," he envisioned Leviathan—a gargantuan, authoritarian state—after the sea creature that swallowed an errant Old Testament prophet as punishment for disobeying God. Whereas Jonah was reprieved, the populace of a Hobbesian state would live out their lives in the belly of the beast—an authoritarian "commonwealth."[12] A ruler should "be their representative," with absolute power to keep order and protect the subjects from both external enemies and their own animal instincts.[13] If individuals had the latitude to determine their rights, mayhem would ensue, and neither state nor the individual would be safe. Therefore, in exchange for order and protection, a subject would have to swear an oath: I give up the right to govern myself.

This compulsory variant of the social contract put Hobbes at odds with the optimistic aspect of the zeitgeist. A prescription for dictatorship, albeit meant to be a benevolent and competent one, did not suit many of the era's intellectuals and reformist politicians. While Hobbes was preparing *Leviathan* for publication, he expected vehement criticism if not outrage from colleagues and successors, and he was not mistaken.[14] It is little wonder that he is often characterized as the Enlightenment's prince of darkness, and his name has come up in academic debates in the early twenty-first century with the rise of "illiberal" democracies, first in central Europe and then in the current American presidency of Donald Trump.

Thomas Hobbes was also controversial, in his own time and beyond, because he doubted that there was a God. In contrast, Baruch Spinoza's concept of God was so radical that even his venturesome and open-minded contemporaries often shied away from him. So did the revolutionaries who would lay the ground for an independent America in the next century.

Spinoza was born in 1632 to a Sephardic family in Amsterdam. His parents had fled the Portuguese Inquisition and settled in the Netherlands during its golden age of culture, global trade, prosperity, and military prowess. Thanks to the Peace of Westphalia, the United Provinces of the Netherlands became an independent republic in the vanguard of religious diversity and free speech. The governors of the provinces—Calvinists in ruffled starched collars—welcomed temporary refugees as well as permanent immigrants, like the Spinozas, who were escaping political heat in their own countries.

When he was twenty-three, Spinoza's synagogue excommunicated him for his audacious insistence that biblical law was not true and God "only existed in the 'philosophical' sense."

So he created his own philosophy for a new definition of God in a ninety-thousand-word treatise titled *Ethics* and circulated it through the Republic of Letters.[15]

Spinoza hewed to a rigorous, deductive, a priori path, moving from definitions and axioms through demonstrated propositions to arrive at the stunning conclusion that God is everything and everywhere, literally and, he was convinced, indisputably. God, he asserted, is not just in every atom, cell, star, thought, event, act of charity or barbarism, pain or joy, truth or lie, human disaster, whether manmade or a new deadly virus. Rather, everything that exists, material or abstract, is in God and, therefore, is God. A bleak thought to many, but not to Spinoza. His signature phrase, "God, or Nature," was not a dichotomy but synonyms to convey one thought—a very big one. God was as impersonal as Nature. "He, who loves God, cannot endeavor that God should love him in return."[16]

There was no heavenly shepherd looking out for mortals and caring for them in the eternal life to come. It was this kind of blunt, unsparing assertion that led the British scholar Jonathan Israel to call Spinoza "the supreme philosophical bogeyman of Early Enlightenment Europe."[17] Steven Nadler takes a more expansive view: "Spinoza has a rightful place among the great philosophers in history. He was certainly the most original, radical, and controversial thinker of his time, and his philosophical, political, and religious ideas laid the foundation for much of what we now regard as 'modern.' "[18]

Spinoza lived during the emergence of deism, a movement that attempted to integrate theology and science, belief and reason. Instead of worshiping the Lord of Heaven and the scriptures, deists accepted a creator of the universe who does not interact with humanity. Although the movement was roundly condemned in the seventeenth century, it appealed to many figures of the European Enlightenment and to many leaders of the American Revolution in the eighteenth.

As Catherine Drinker Bowen wrote in *The Miracle at Philadelphia*, her widely read account of the Constitutional Convention in 1787: "Deism was in the air. Two generations ago it had made the westward crossing, to the immense perturbation of the faithful. Here was a religion free of creed: the Newtonian universe, the classical revival, the discovery of new seas and new lands had enlarged the world but crowded the old dogma rudely."[19]

Spinoza, who crowded it more rudely than anyone, remained a name that was rarely whispered except by the bravest freethinkers (Franklin, Adams, and Jefferson). It took the German Enlightenment in the eighteenth century and its Jewish spin-off to appreciate where Spinoza's relentless logic had taken him. On both sides of the Atlantic in the nineteenth century, some Jewish congregations treated Spinoza with the same interest and respect as they did Maimonides.[20]

Modern deists often claim Albert Einstein as one of their own. He demurred, being drawn instead to the outcast Jew who posited divinity not as a supreme being but as the essence of all creation existing in nature, animate or otherwise. This would encourage Einstein to pursue the unified field theory even though it remained elusive—or perhaps because it was elusive. Spinoza's God could coexist with Einstein's universe.[21]

———

In contrast with Spinoza's mind-bending metaphysics, his views on liberal government were down-to-earth. They were also ahead of his time. More than most Enlightenment philosophers, he studied the masses, combining empathy for the downtrodden and awareness of the danger to society if they were ignored. In

Ethics, he urged the political powers and the intelligentsia to pay attention to the populace's emotions, especially their fear and frustration.

He elaborated in the *Theologico-Political Treatise*, one of his works published in his lifetime: "In a Free Republic everyone is permitted to think what he wishes and to say what he thinks."[22] In this work, published anonymously, Spinoza also defended freedom of speech as a corollary to sovereignty of the individual: "If, then, no one can surrender his freedom of judging and thinking what he wishes, but everyone, by the greatest natural right, is master of his own thoughts, it follows that if the supreme powers in a republic try to make men say nothing but what they prescribe, no matter how different and contrary their opinions, they will get only the most unfortunate result."[23] Moreover, if the authorities of the state tried to muzzle free expression, it would backfire, possibly in rebellion: "It simply couldn't happen that everyone spoke within prescribed limits. On the contrary, the more the authorities try to take away this freedom of speech, the more stubbornly men will resist."[24]

Elsewhere, he reiterated the key component of a social contract: "The end of the Republic . . . is not to change men from rational beings into beasts or automata, but to enable their minds and bodies to perform their functions safely, to enable them to use their reason freely, and not to clash with one another in hatred, anger, or deception, or deal inequitably with one another."[25]

Ever the realist, he urged that a sturdy government must have enough processes and institutions to survive periods of malfeasance: "For a [state] to be able to last, its affairs must be so ordered that, whether the people who administer them are led by reason or by an affect, they can't be induced to be disloyal or to act badly."[26]

By "administration," Spinoza meant sturdy institutions of government that would restrain incompetent, harmful, or overbearing rulers. This principle would find its way into the heart of the American Constitution in the form of federalism and separation of powers.

———

Spinoza was a liberal with no romantic illusions of rebellion or populist rule. If the populace is ignored, upheaval will ensue: "Tyranny is most violent where individual beliefs, which are an inalienable right, are regarded as criminal. Indeed, in such circumstances, the anger of the mob is usually the greatest tyrant of all."[27]

His advice for dealing with populists and their adherents reads well today: elites should get over their snobbish notion that the hoi polloi are ignorant and unfit to judge what is good for the polity or themselves. "[E]veryone shares a common nature," he asserted, suggesting that elitism was a dubious category, especially if the intellectual class determined what was good for the "inferiors."[28]

In this regard, Spinoza was wary of his own profession. If his fellow philosophers in their cloisters continued to extol cool reason and dismiss the passions of the crowds on the streets, as was their wont, they would stir up resentment and incite demagoguery. To avert that, he put the onus on government and the elites themselves. In their civic roles, they should study the people's lives and needs.

Spinoza's quest took him to a distant, lonely corner of the philosophical universe in a relatively short life. He died at the age of forty-four, about the average lifespan of a seventeenth-century European.[29] In death, he would become part of God/Nature. A passage from the *Ethics* serves as a fitting epitaph: "A free man thinks of death least of all things, and his wisdom is to meditate not on death but on life."[30] It took several generations for Spinoza to be widely rediscovered, mainly in the nineteenth and twentieth centuries, and, in some cases, reinterpreted for purposes that would be alien to his philosophy.[31]

———

John Locke was born the same year as Spinoza and shared fundamental beliefs with this bold outsider, notably the inalienable rights of all human beings, including the right to rebel against tyranny. However, Locke was a proper Anglican. He welcomed the patronage of aristocrats, who, in turn, might have looked dubiously on his work had they known Locke was influenced by a renegade Jew with a reputation as a pagan.[32]

While Spinoza was a shooting star in the firmament of the Enlightenment, Locke's ascent started gradually. After studying medicine at Oxford, Locke entered an upper-class medical practice before turning to epistemology and political philosophy. He wrote slowly, meticulously, and prolifically. And because of the dangerous Stuart reign, with its entangled power plays between Crown and Parliament and between Protestantism and a revived Catholicism, he wrote discreetly, encrypting his notes and hiding manuscripts in a secret compartment of his desk. Such precautions did not, however, remove him from suspicions that he was plotting against the Crown, so Locke slipped off to Holland, the most liberal nation in Europe.

Algernon Sidney, a reformist parliamentarian and political theorist, was protesting the divine right of kings, much as Locke made that case in the same period. But Sidney was less discreet and fortunate. In 1683 he was accused of conspiring to assassinate Charles II. He was arrested, and a draft of his treatise justifying revolution was confiscated.[33] Sentencing Sidney to death, the presiding judge proclaimed "Scribere est agere" (To write is to act). Sidney's response from the scaffold resonates today: "We live in an age that makes truth pass for treason."

Locke's self-exile in his fifties could have been an anticlimax to what seemed a middling career: a lapsed physician turned into a brilliant but skittish philosopher. Most of the evidence of his genius was in his head or squirreled away. As he contemplated old age, he saw little chance of returning to England, nor could he be sure that several projects he had been working on for nearly two decades would ever be read. Although he was sufficiently comfortable and safe, he seemed unmoored, spending time "much in my chamber alone," sitting by a fire, reading, and corresponding with friends in a homeland he might never see again.[34] And though he returned to medicine, his passion would always remain the study of the mind.

———

When Charles II died in 1685, the Crown passed to his stunningly inept brother, James II, who wasted no time making powerful enemies. He raised suspicions that he intended to roll back Parliament's hard-won prerogatives, infuriated the Anglican establishment by promoting his fellow Catholics to high posts, and sidled up to Britain's archrival, France. After four tumultuous years, James was deposed and replaced by his Protestant daughter, Mary, keeping the Stuart dynasty on the throne. Mary, in turn, insisted that her husband, William of Orange, join her as co-monarch, adding to his status as stadholder (effectively, chief executive and commander of five Dutch Republic provinces) the title King of England, Scotland, and Ireland.

Convoluted as this maneuver was, the reigning couple brought to English politics a measure of stability and liberalism—two trends that do not always come in tandem. It was now possible for Locke to return home and publish his books.

In his masterwork, *An Essay concerning Human Understanding*, Locke rejected the concept of "native ideas" stamped "upon [our] minds, in their very first being."[35] The mind at birth is a *tabula rasa*, he believed—a "white paper, void of all characters, without any ideas."[36]

Rationality, he concluded, was an innate human faculty that produces ideas as we accumulate knowledge through experience: "Reason must be our last judge and guide in everything."[37] By studying our environment and exercising rationality in our own lives, we gain the capacity and incentive to form ideas on how to cope with the opportunities and challenges of life.[38]

———

Locke, along with many of his contemporaries, believed that happiness—or at least an environment in which it could be pursued—was a perquisite for an enlightened polity and society. "Nature, I confess, has put into man a desire of happiness, and an aversion to misery: these indeed are innate practical principles, which (as practical principles ought) do continue constantly to operate and influence all our actions without ceasing: These may be observ'd in all Persons and all Ages, steady and universal."[39]

In present-day English, *happiness* usually carries the connotation of personal good fortune or contentment, fleeting or otherwise. But, in the seventeenth and eighteenth centuries, philosophers gave it added moral weight. Happiness should be the result of altruism and empathy. A worthy person should care for the happiness of others, and an enlightened government should care for the collective happiness and prosperity of society as a whole.

———

Locke had been revising the *Essay* for almost a decade before he launched into *Two Treatises of Government*. It would not be published until 1689 and even then, anonymously. Despite growing tolerance following the Glorious Revolution, Locke knew his ideas were ahead of his time and therefore dangerous.

The *Two Treatises* was a model social contract between the governors and the governed. He considered rationality, tolerance, and happiness critical for both. Whether surveying the world around us or probing inward to understand our minds, we are each a monarch unto ourselves, entitled to personal liberty in thought, belief, persuasion, religion, and speech.[40]

Locke denounced "received doctrines" such as the divine right of kings. He asserted that all individuals are free—and, moreover, obligated—to use their wits to understand the world and cope with it ethically.

Locke, Hobbes, and Spinoza believed that, in nature, there was no such thing as right or wrong, virtue or sin. It was incumbent upon the state to set rules and to enforce them with punishment or reward. Hobbes did not trust the Leviathan's subjects to have leverage over their government, whereas Locke (like Spinoza) insisted the opposite. Hobbes believed an authoritarian regime would, inevitably, repress its subjects, whereas an enlightened government would respect the inborn, inherent rights of its citizens: "Being all equal and independent, no one ought to harm another in his life, health, liberty, or possessions."[41]

No one meant no one, including the ruler of the state. In the *Second Treatise*, Locke rejected the belief that the divine creator of the universe also judged the affairs of "man," and he insisted that man-made law must be based on due processes of government and legislature. This assertion that an abusive monarch is an illegitimate one is essentially the same argument that cost Algernon Sidney his head. It also inspired the American founders to risk their own lives, fortunes, and sacred honor.

———

Locke's *An Essay concerning Human Understanding* also endorsed separation of religion and politics in a chapter titled "Of Faith and Reason, and their Distinct Provinces." He knew both provinces and was clear about their differences and their boundaries.[42] While a dedicated rationalist, he was also a member of the Church of England who was well-read in the Bible. His letters from Holland to friends in England suggest that excluding accounts of supernatural events, he had found wisdom in both the Old and New Testaments. He had faith in God but would never try to persuade others to do likewise, since he could offer no proof of the deity's existence.

Back in the Province of Reason, Locke could explain and defend his propositions with evidence and logic. Authorities could enact laws and create institutions as long as they did not intrude into the private chapel of the mind. During the first four years after his return to England, he wrote *A Letter concerning Toleration*, laying down a broad admonition to any government: "The care of each man's soul, and of the things of heaven, which neither does belong to the commonwealth nor can be subjected to it, is left entirely to every man's self."[43]

Locke believed that no "judge on earth"—rulers and lawmakers—possessed the capacity to pronounce verdicts on spiritual matters.[44] For that reason alone, officials of the state had no business forcing citizens to adopt a "true religion" while suppressing adherents of other faiths.[45]

———

Publishing the *Two Treatises of Government* anonymously may not have been necessary, given how little notice it received. The British historian John Kenyon writes that Locke's ideas were mentioned rarely in the early stages of the Glorious Revolution, up to 1692, "and even less thereafter, unless it was to heap abuse on them."[46]

The aging philosopher ached with disappointment as he approached the end of his life. He saw himself as a second-tier figure in the eyes of his contemporaries and likely to be unknown in the future. According to his *Essay*, when he scanned the landscape of "the commonwealth of learning," he saw "masterbuilders, whose mighty designs, in advancing the sciences, will leave lasting monuments to the admiration of posterity." He singled out Isaac Newton, whose discovery of the laws of nature put him in the first rank of physics, astronomy, mathematics, optics, and cosmology. Comparing himself with Newton, Locke was, he said, "an under-labourer in clearing the ground a little, and removing some of the rubbish that lies in the way to knowledge."[47] Locke's reputation as a master designer of republican government reached its apex well after his death. The Declaration of Independence embraced the concept that all human beings are equal at birth and have unalienable liberties, one of which is the pursuit of happiness. Locke made the argument for the right of revolt against an unjust ruler. The Constitution endorsed Locke's rationale for separating the branches of government, and the Bill of Rights echoed his promotion of freedom of speech, press, peaceable assembly, and petition for grievances.

The founders of the United States of America were intensely aware that among those Englishmen who prepared the philosophical ground with ideas and ideals for a revolution, a government, and a new kind of nation, Locke had the most influence.

However, Bernard Bailyn, in *The Ideological Origins of the American Revolution*, lays down a caveat to the loose bond between the thinkers of the Old World and the doers of the New World: "The leaders of resistance . . . were not philosophers. . . . They did not write for formal discourses, nor did they feel bound to adhere to traditional political maxims or to apparently logical reasoning that led to conclusions they feared."[48]

Moreover, the founders owed a deeper debt to their American ancestors who, in the seventeenth century, braved months at sea, settled for the rest of their lives in a new world, and, unknowingly, spread seeds of a new country.

3

An Errand in the Wilderness

America [is] the only country in which the starting point
of a great people has been clearly observable.

—*Alexis de Tocqueville*

Most of the first British settlers on the North Atlantic seaboard came to the New World because they were impoverished, persecuted, fleeing from the law, or alienated from family, society, or politics. Although they were subjects of the Crown, they welcomed its distance.

In 1607 three ships owned by the Virginia Company dropped anchor off the banks of the James River, near the mouth of the Chesapeake Bay. About a hundred passengers, most of whom would never see England again, founded Jamestown, named after the Stuart monarch of the day. They were male and mostly adventurers. Not until the following year did women arrive: a Mistress Forrest and her maid, Anne Burras, followed by a few more a year later, including Temperance Flowerdew, the wife of Captain George Yeardley, who later became governor of the colony. They were a pitiful but vital addition to what would be the first permanent British colony in the Americas. In 1619 the company recruited about 150 Englishwomen to travel to the colony and wed the males. These brave, poor, and desperate volunteers, while compensated for their journey, were unprepared for the hardships at sea and those at their destination.

Within a few years, many died from starvation or disease, or in raids by indigenous people.[1]

The charge from James I was threefold: Create a settlement on the southern Atlantic coast as a buffer against Spanish conquistadors encroaching on what would be British America; reap the bounty of the land—gold and silver was the hope, but tobacco was the bonanza; and convert to Christianity the descendants of clans who had lived in that hemisphere tens of thousands of years before Europeans sailed into their world.

The first two goals were, after many setbacks, successful, but the third was a grotesque charade and failure. Few natives joined the Church of England, and many resisted the white man's incursions. They were experienced warriors whose arrows, spears, and tomahawks might have outmatched the invaders, especially when the tribes captured and bought guns. But they were not armed with European immunities against European diseases. They succumbed quickly up and down the Atlantic seaboard. By some estimates, 90 percent of the coastal indigenous population died from alien microbes.

Twelve years after the founding of Jamestown, a British privateer, the *White Lion*, attacked the *São João Bautista*, a Portuguese slave ship, off the coast of New Spain (now Mexico). The British seized the human cargo, consisting of twenty captives from the Kingdom of Ndongo, a region in what is today Angola. They were sold into bondage to work in the tobacco fields in the Virginia Colony.[2]

Two infamies inflicted on people of different color stained the American soul and soil for centuries to come.

More than a decade later, in 1620, a new wave of settlers set forth for New England. They called themselves Pilgrims, a radical off-shoot of Puritanism, which rose out of the Protestant Reformation in Europe. The Pilgrims were passionately and inflexibly pious or, as they said, godly. In their eyes, mainstream Anglicanism had relapsed into worldliness and, worse, into corrupt Catholic prac-tices. Their mission was to establish a place where their "true" religion could flourish, unimpeded by magistrates who served the king and the Church of England, now an ocean away.

The Pilgrims who sailed on the *Mayflower* to establish the Plymouth Colony had made a permanent break from England and had rejected the church that bore its name. After another ten years, mainstream Puritans came to Massachusetts, bent on reforming—that is, purifying—Anglicanism. Both sects were followers of John Calvin, the charismatic, fiercely unbending French reformer whose theology, an offshoot of Martin Luther's, emphasized God's sovereignty, teaching his followers that only those elected by Him would find salvation in eternity.[3]

The Puritans had maintained an uneasy truce with King James I, but his successor, Charles I, was a threat to their com-munity and religion. As royal intolerance intensified to oppres-sion and persecution, they looked for guidance in the Bible. For many, the Book of Exodus provided an answer. They would put an ocean between themselves and an earthly sovereign. That would allow them to be the masters of their own land and ser-vants of their Lord.

Unlike the Jewish people in their Egyptian captivity, the Puritans did not think of themselves as turning their backs on an alien land. Rather, they set off to New England to keep the flame of their faith burning until they could return to Old England after it had become purified under a Puritan government. Their sojourn came to be called an "errand into the wilderness." Their errand was not intended to be forever; when finished, they expected, they would go home.[4]

Even though they were increasingly out of favor with King James, the Puritans were well established in English business circles. Under their influence, a commercial venture in Massachusetts Bay was reorganized as a colony. The company's directors hoodwinked His Britannic Majesty by presenting him a prolix charter that was larded with scrapes and bows to the throne. The numbing verbiage seems to have camouflaged a deliberate omission: there was no mention of where the annual stockholders' meeting would be held in the future. That sleight of pen permitted the directors to move the seat of governance from London to the colony itself, thereby weakening the control of the Crown.[5]

———

The principal agent of that step toward quasi-independence was John Winthrop, the first leader of the Massachusetts Bay Colony. In that capacity, he was both a holdout of a vanishing system of governance—religious patriarchy—and an experimenter of proto-republicanism.

He arrived in an eleven-vessel fleet in 1630, leading a flock of more than seven hundred to their new home. The Great Puritan Migration was underway.

Winthrop's fame today comes largely from a sermon titled "A Model of Christian Charity" that he reputedly wrote aboard the *Arbella*, the flagship of the flotilla. Yet there are no known contemporaneous sources that would fix a date and a place where he might have delivered it, or how it was received, or whether he delivered it at all. For all we know, Winthrop's message bypassed his seagoing parish and went right into a time capsule, widely unknown for three centuries, until his prophecy became a paean to a strong, righteous example of the world during the Cold War and after. In 1989 Andrew Delbanco, a professor of American studies at Columbia, consecrated it as "a kind of Ur-text" of the national narrative.[6]

Of the some six thousand words Winthrop composed, a single sentence was elevated to a place in U.S. presidential rhetoric in the twentieth and twenty-first centuries: "We must consider that we shall be as a city upon a hill. The eyes of all people are upon us."[7] John Kennedy made it a bipartisan trope for his successors to invoke America's moral strength, magnanimity, optimism, championship of liberty, and leadership in the world. Ronald Reagan picked it up, as did Barack Obama.

———

Winthrop's immediate, practical, and somber purpose was to fortify his fellow passengers' faith that the Lord would protect them in the face of certain and unknown perils. His message was one of pride, responsibility, and liberation. As the Puritans waited for the purification of the Church of England and England itself, Winthrop loosened the rule of the colony from London by moving its seat from Salem to Charlestown without royal permission. This ploy gave the Puritans a latent, subtle advance in the direction of self-governance.[8]

While future generations came to revere Winthrop as an inspiring orator, in his own time he earned respect for his leadership in his alternating terms as governor and lieutenant governor of Massachusetts over twenty years. He exercised a firm but moderate and fair hand in an era of authoritarianism, initiating several features of governance that would serve the United States a century later. He reined in zealotry among the clergy and respected the laity's consent for the laws of the community by encouraging petitioning and participation in civil debates.[9]

As governor, Winthrop was no democrat by today's definition, nor was he a despot. The minutes of the first meeting in Charlestown suggest that he invited male members of the community to attend the sessions and voice their reactions to the decisions. The outcome of the meeting "was fully assented unto by the general vote of the people."[10]

Winthrop rejected "mere"—that is, direct—democracy, but he had laid the ground for the representative, or indirect, variant that the founders would favor.[11]

John Winthrop was one of the most judicious and esteemed conservatives in the New England hierarchy, and Roger Williams—a courageous, passionate radical—was one of the most controversial.

Before joining the Great Migration, Williams believed that Puritanism needed to be cleansed of corruption and made more inclusive. He had no patience with the idea that Puritans were the vanguard of the Church of England. Much as the Pilgrim separatists, he wanted a clean split from Anglicanism.

Williams was the ultimate freethinker who scandalized much of the community by openly expressing his personal convictions with ferocious eloquence, particularly when he was railing against efforts to impose how people should pray: "Forced worship stinks in God's nostrils."[12] He had his God, others had theirs. He joined the Baptist branch of Protestantism, which shared his toleration of other sects.

Williams was unswerving in his own faith, and he was certain that those of other denominations were destined to hell. But that ultimate judgment was for God to make. He was also convinced that mortals were unable to interpret God's law wisely; when they tried, they distorted its meaning, stumbling into earthly injustice. From that premise, he opposed—loudly and often—theocracy in general, and any government involvement in religious affairs. He denounced the concept of Christendom, since it was a political domain of the church, and scoffed at the British Crown's claim to jurisdiction over the settlements in North America.

He had left England several months after the *Arbella* flo-tilla, arriving in Massachusetts in early 1631. He spent five years in the Bay Colony, quickly earning a reputation as a gadfly on many issues, especially the settlers' cruel treatment of the Native Americans. He chided his fellow Englishmen for bigotry and rejected a law that permitted the eviction of natives from their villages and hunting grounds. He was put on trial for "diverse, new, and dangerous opinions," charges that amounted to sedition and heresy.[13]

Winthrop disagreed with almost all of Williams's unortho-dox ideas and concurred with the General Court's decision to expel him from the Bay Colony. Nevertheless, Winthrop sug-gested that Williams turn ignominy into opportunity: he should move to Narragansett Bay, neighboring the Massachusetts Bay Colony, for "high and heavenly and public ends."[14] Williams took the advice and founded the colony of Rhode Island as a haven for those "distressed for conscience." He stood his ground on expansive religious tolerance:

> There goes many a ship to sea, with many hundred souls in one ship, whose weal and woe is common, and is a true picture of a commonwealth or a human combination or so-ciety. It hath fallen out sometimes that Papists, Protestants, Jews, and Turks may be embarked in one ship; upon which supposal I affirm that all the liberty of conscience that ever I pleaded for turns upon these two hinges: that none of the Papists, Protestants, Jews, or Turks be forced to come to the ships' prayers or worship, nor be compelled [restrained]

from their own particular prayers or worship, if they practice any.[15]

Williams's notoriety reached John Locke, who was impressed by this fearless promoter of religious toleration. Locke was a thinker, while Williams was a doer, pushing for colonial laws that embodied liberal values—much to the horror and disgust of his fellow governors.[16]

Williams's own errand in the wilderness carried a stunning portent of America's destiny. He leaped ahead of the abstract thinkers back in the land of his birth, transforming their ideas into a whole new way of governing. He guided Rhode Island wisely and compassionately, under the authority of a charter to establish religious freedom, the first in the New World.[17]

He was an early convert to the cause of abolition of slavery and taught himself several tribal languages to enable him to cooperate fairly with Native Americans. Celebrated and detested, in life and after his death at seventy-nine, he was one of America's first liberals, long before that hardy skein was woven into the American political tapestry.

Despite the religious, ethical, and political gulf between Williams and Winthrop, the radical considered the conservative a friend who offered him a new opportunity to pursue his mission. For years after their parting, Williams kept up a correspondence with Winthrop, effusive with gratitude and respect.[18]

That Williams could move to another jurisdiction more receptive to his views was an option unlikely to be found in England. This demonstrated yet another advantage of the dan-

gerous, hardscrabble, and vast New World: it was far more ac-
commodating to individualists.

————

Anne Hutchinson was among those intrepid, strong-minded figures. Like Williams, she was a deeply religious maverick and
crusader for those who shared her ideas about worship and salvation. And, like Williams, she came under fire for challenging
the authority of the Puritan church. But unlike Williams, she
became a fierce and lasting enemy of Winthrop.[19]

Despite the disapproval of the authorities, she ministered
to women in Boston, first as a nurse and midwife, providing
care for those who were sick or in labor. She held meetings at
her home so women of the community could discuss the week's
sermon, pray together, and enjoy a rare opportunity to social-
ize.[20] Hutchinson's gatherings soon attracted people from surrounding villages, who came to hear her divergent religious views
and critiques of the local ministers' sermons. To Winthrop's fury,
prominent townsmen became curious and began to attend, dis-
rupting what Locke called the "received doctrines." Hutchinson
preached that salvation was received "not by conduct, not by
obeying the commandments, by giving alms, praying, fasting or
wearing a long face." Instead, she urged accepting "God's spirit
within," much along the lines of Williams's freethinking.[21]

Hutchinson was bound to get into trouble, and Winthrop
was the chief prosecutor for her trial on charges of speaking
"in derogation of the ministers" of the colony and "[troubling]

the peace of the commonwealth and churches." She handled her own defense vigorously, matching her all-male interrogators in her knowledge of scripture and church doctrine. But when Hutchinson referred to her "immediate revelation"—a personal communication from God, who vowed to curse the Puritans and their descendants if they harmed her—the judges pounced, charging that she was a danger to civil order and "a woman not fit for our society."[22] The verdict echoes down the centuries of misogyny in America. Today she might be shunned as a "nasty woman."

When she was exiled from Massachusetts, Roger Williams invited Hutchinson and her husband William, a former member of the General Court, her younger children (she had fifteen, with the older ones back in England), and a group of followers to settle in Rhode Island. There she found more than refuge: she became the first—and last—female cofounder of an American colony.[23]

Even after Hutchinson left the Massachusetts Bay Colony, Winthrop kept track of her so he could vilify her from afar. When he learned that she had suffered a molar pregnancy, he declared, "See how the wisdom of God fitted this judgement to her sin every way, for look as she had vented mishapen opinions, so she must bring forth deformed monsters."[24]

When Hutchinson's enemies in Boston threatened a takeover of Rhode Island, she moved her family down the coast, near New Amsterdam, a town on the southern tip of Manhattan Island where Dutch settlers congregated. The Dutch colony was in a simmering conflict with a local tribe. In 1643 it boiled over. Hutchinson and all but one of the younger members of her family who were living with her perished in a massacre aimed at terrorizing the white settlers. When word reached the Bay Colony, its leaders saw it as the "just vengeance of God."[25] Winthrop concurred.

Three hundred years later, Eleanor Roosevelt extolled Hutchinson as the first of America's foremothers—and literally so, since she was an ancestor of Franklin D. Roosevelt and George H. W. and George W. Bush.[26]

———

John Winthrop's health declined on the threshold of his seventh decade. When he died peacefully, still in office, he was widely mourned. The same could not be said of the Puritans' royal nemesis. Two months before Winthrop's death, King Charles I had been beheaded for treason. His marriage to a French Catholic princess had stirred protests among Anglicans and other Protestants, and his claim of absolute power under the divine right of kings clashed with the English and Scottish Parliaments, who were jealous of their own prerogatives.

Civil war erupted in 1642, ending with Charles's defeat and capture. He refused demands for a constitutional monarchy, and he spent most of his last days imprisoned on the Isle of Wight, where the *Arbella* and its fleet had set sail nineteen years earlier. He was executed on January 30, 1649.

The principal signatory of the warrant for the king's execution was Oliver Cromwell. As Lord Protector of the Commonwealth of England, Scotland, and Ireland, he was the most powerful Puritan of all time and virtual dictator of the country that Winthrop and others had left for a new life in a new land.

Crossings of the Atlantic were slower and more dangerous in winter, so when the news of the regicide arrived, many of the members of the Great Migration rejoiced. Winthrop's son Stephen returned to England to serve in Cromwell's government. John Endecott and Richard Bellingham, then governor and deputy governor, respectively, of the Bay Colony, wrote to Cromwell, thanking him for his "continued series of favours" to "us poor exiles, in these utmost ends of the earth."[27]

———

The Cromwell Protectorate had lasted only six years before it collapsed, soon after Cromwell's death in 1658. His son and successor, Richard, was ousted by the military, and the royalists returned to power. Now it was Cromwell's turn to be convicted of treason, albeit posthumously. His body was disinterred from Westminster Abbey and hanged, by tradition, on the Tyburn gallows for the public to gawk and cheer, "Long live the King!"

When news of the latest upheaval reached the Puritans in America, many must have begun to question whether God still planned for their progeny to return to rule England. But they took comfort in the survival of their own venture, and saw more clearly the opportunities of this new land. The wilderness seemed less wild and their errand less transient. More and more, they were concentrating on how to govern themselves.[28]

In February 1660, Charles II sent greetings and assurances from the throne to his subjects in Massachusetts:

> We have made it our care to settle our lately distracted kingdoms at home, and to extend our thoughts to increase the trade and advantages of our colonies and plantations abroad. Amongst which as we consider New-England to be one of the chiefest, having enjoyed and grown up in a long and orderly establishment, so we shall not come behind any of our royal predecessors in a just encouragement and protection of all our loving subjects there. . . . We are confident our good subjects in New-England will make a right use of it, to the glory of God, their own spiritual comfort and edification. And so we bid you farewell.[29]

Farewell indeed. In the following decades, as the world left the seventeenth century, North America was loosening its lifelines from Britain. Younger Puritans were less Puritan—that is, less godly—than their elders.

The Salem witch trials in 1692 and 1693 marked the demise of Puritanism. Earlier ministers and magistrates of Winthrop's ilk had refuted and quietly dismissed accusations of witchcraft.[30] The trials had a profound effect on religion in America. George Lincoln Burr—a prominent American educator, librarian, and historian who, in the late nineteenth century, compiled a collection of rare books on the subject—wrote that the mass hysteria followed by brutal executions was "the rock on which the theocracy shattered."[31]

Joseph J. Ellis credits the "gallery of greats" of the last quarter of the eighteenth century with making sure that theocracy stayed in crumbles: The founders "created the first wholly secular state. Before the American founding, it was assumed that state support for an established religion was a mandatory feature of all viable governments because it enforced a consensus on the common values that made a collective sense of purpose possible."[32]

———

But before turning to extraordinary events in the future, there must be a coda in a minor key.

At least two heroes of the seventeenth-century English Enlightenment were not yet enlightened when they turned their inquiring minds to the New World. Thomas Hobbes and John Locke ran afoul of their intellectual and moral standards. They were caught up in bigotry on the issue of race—and, in particular, toward Native Americans and African slaves.

Hobbes, when active in the Virginia Company in the 1620s, received wildly distorted and self-serving reports from the colonial and commercial officials about the barbarity of the Native Americans and the unprovoked mayhem they were inflicting on the peaceable settlers. He took this propaganda at face value, as evidence that the Native Americans had to be tamed by stern but benevolent rulers from advanced societies. In *Leviathan*, he wrote: "For the savage people in many places of America, except the government of small families, the concord whereof dependeth on natural lust, have no government at all; and live at this day in that brutish manner."[33]

When Locke was commissioned to oversee laws for the Carolina colony, he, too, was also gulled by the white man's propaganda. Later, in *Two Treatises of Government*, he mused on what he had been told about the natives three thousand miles away. He portrayed Native Americans as primitives living in a primeval state of nature, acquiring or disposing of possessions "without asking leave, or depending upon the will of any other man"—what civilized people would call lawlessness and rampant crime.[34] While Hobbes was fixated on a lack of government and morals among the savages, Locke concluded they had no money and no laws.

These two eminent English empiricists were just plain wrong. Over the millennia, Native American tribes had developed intricate political institutions, laws, and—yes—money. If Hobbes and Locke had been accurately apprised of the facts, they would have recognized a complex empire encompassing much of Virginia, Chesapeake Bay, and southern Maryland. Powhatan, a potentate who presided over numerous Algonquian-speaking tribes, wanted to trade with the English when Jamestown was first settled, before it became clear that the newcomers were there to stay and bent on usurping the land.[35]

A pithy statement in Locke's *Two Treatises of Government* has been much quoted: "In the beginning all the World was

America," leading a reader to infer, mistakenly, that Locke was speculating that the Western Hemisphere was the anthropological birthplace of humanity.[36]

Homo sapiens, according to twentieth-century science, emerged in the savannas of Africa. Several millenniums later, enslaved people from that continent would soon join the indigenous people in America, where they, too, would suffer an ongoing catastrophe.

When wrestling with the issue of race and bondage, both philosophers resorted to casuistry to defend the absurdity that slaves bought in Africa and sold in British colonies were prisoners of war.[37] Locke seemed to be more conflicted than Hobbes, perhaps because he was more liberal.[38] He argued both sides of the case, condemning the practice and then, in the same treatise, suggesting that circumstances justified it. In the late 1660s, he oversaw the drafting of the constitution for the Province of Carolina, which proclaimed, "Every Freeman of Carolina shall have absolute power and Authority over his Negro slaves."[39] Moreover, Locke was a shareholder in the Royal African Company, which shipped human cargo from the Gold Coast of Africa to the West Indies.[40]

He profited, along with countless others, from the delivery of thousands of Africans whose offspring would toil on plantations, such as George Washington's Mount Vernon on the Potomac and Thomas Jefferson's Monticello in the Blue Ridge Mountains. From there, they would spread out into America as it expanded. In time, the descendants of the original slaves became free citizens in the eyes of the law, but the law often looked away when whites subjugated and humiliated them, reminding them of the scars of their shackles from the Middle Passage and the whips of their ancestors' masters.

Locke contributed profoundly to the American Enlightenment, but he was also complicit in its greatest failing.[41]

4

Books from Beyond the Sea

I give to my son, when he shall arrive to the age of fifteen
years, Algernon Sidney's works, John Locke's works, Lord
Bacon's works, Gordon's *Tacitus*, and *Cato's Letters*.
May the spirit of liberty rest upon him.

—*Josiah Quincy Jr.*

The band of British colonists who created the United States of America stretched across nearly a century and a half, from the firstborn, Benjamin Franklin, to the last to die, John Quincy Adams. Those two, like most of the others in between, were more than acquaintances; they were principals in a great drama, and their roles were linked. So were their intellectual lives, which intertwined with their political lives. It was no small piquancy, if not irony, that British philosophers helped light the fire of rebellion.

A death and a birth could serve as a metaphor for the Enlightenment's leap across the Atlantic. At seventy-two, John Locke expired in the Essex countryside in 1704. Two years later, Franklin came squalling into a world that he would help enliven and change as the archdruid of the American Enlightenment.

Locke's understanding of the human mind contributed to the liberalization of government beyond the horizon of his own life, while Franklin's utilitarianism, scope of genius, and political and diplomatic skills put him in the leadership of the American experiment at its most formative and most precarious phase.

Locke had the educational and professional advantages of

the English upper classes. If Franklin had been born on London's Grub Street or in St. Giles Parish, odds would have been against his ascendency to the British hierarchy. Instead, he was delivered in a modest cottage, crowded with siblings, on Boston's Milk Street in a working-class neighborhood.

The Massachusetts Bay Colony was growing too rapidly for a rigid caste system to have formed. Franklin personified a generation that established America's middle-class meritocracy, a generation with more access to Old World knowledge than their ancestors in the previous century.[1]

When John Winthrop sailed into Salem Harbor aboard the *Arbella* in 1630, he brought with him some fifty books, mostly bibles and theological tracts. Seventy years later, a thousand vessels were registered in Boston, most carrying all kinds of reading matter from Britain and other European countries.[2] Shipyards on both sides of the ocean were thriving. Improvements in marine technology and navigation meant faster and safer passages.[3] British publishers found the colonials eager for newspapers, political tracts, and books that brought new ways of thinking, praying, preaching, storytelling, living, and governing. For the first six decades of the eighteenth century, controversial pamphlets available on Fleet Street in London or High Street in Oxford were likely to find their way to the New World.

In the English-speaking world, only London, Dublin, and Edinburgh had more bookshops than Boston.[4] The demand from the American colonies was as robust as the supply. Unwittingly, the mother country was educating her children on the other side of the Atlantic in the ways of reform and protest.

Among Franklin's wide-ranging enthusiasms, one that he held dear was the power of the printed word. In his public service, philanthropy, and science, he was constantly looking for new ways to ensure that this upstart outpost of Western civilization would be renowned for widespread literacy. He knew that education was indispensable for an enlightened society—and, when the colonies became a republic, for a responsible electorate.[5]

———

Reading was young Benjamin's first sign of precociousness. He owed that to his father, Josiah, a soap and candle maker who came to America in the latter phase of the Great Puritan Migration. Along with others, he was motivated by economic opportunity and escape from sectarian restrictions.[6]

As Josiah expanded his business and family in Boston (Benjamin was the third to last of his father's seventeen children), this self-educated tradesman reserved a shelf for books that he prized. As Benjamin recounted in his autobiography decades later, "My father's little library consisted chiefly of books in polemic divinity, most of which I read, and have since often regretted that, at a time when I had such a thirst for knowledge, more proper books had not fallen in my way, since it was now resolved I should not be a clergyman."[7]

Much more to his liking was *Pilgrim's Progress* by John Bunyan, himself an important contributor to the Enlightenment. Although the story too had a religious theme, it bore no resemblance to the dry homilies in Josiah's collection.

Bunyan was among English writers who, toward the end of the seventeenth century, breathed new life into fiction. In *Pilgrim's Progress*, rather than retelling the familiar biblical parables, he took his readers on an action-packed, phantasmagorical quest to find the Celestial City. Along the way, the hero, Christian, encounters angels, devils, monsters, and "the Slough of Despond" that sucks sinners into a bottomless bog. Bunyan let his imagination soar, inviting his readers to join the flight, entertaining and edifying them. The Celestial City was far from Winthrop's "City upon a Hill."

Walter Isaacson speculates that Franklin might have found, hidden in the miracles and flights of fancy in this religious allegory, a homespun revelation that would resonate in his own life: "A central theme of Bunyan's book—and of the passage from Puritanism to Enlightenment, and of Franklin's life—was contained in its title: *progress*, the concept that individuals, and humanity in general, move forward and improve based on a steady increase of knowledge and the wisdom that comes from conquering adversity."[8]

After finishing the book, Franklin—ever frugal—sold it to purchase Richard Burton's collection of adventures and travelogues, a book about real events and earthly journeys. He was already a history buff.[9] His father had a worn copy of Plutarch's *Lives* on his shelf. Franklin noted in his autobiography, "I read it abundantly."[10]

Daniel Defoe's first notable work, *An Essay upon Projects*, also drew Benjamin to another treasure on Josiah's bookshelf.

Defoe's title itself might have had a lure, and the first paragraph must have hooked his young reader:

> Necessity, which is allowed to be the mother of invention, has so violently agitated the wits of men at this time that it seems not at all improper, by way of distinction, to call it the Projecting Age. For though in times of war and public confusions the like humour of invention has seemed to stir, yet, without being partial to the present, it is, I think, no injury to say the past ages have never come up to the degree of projecting and inventing, as it refers to matters of negotiation and methods of civil polity, which we see this age arrived to.[11]

The "projecting age," even though the phrase never caught on, captured the Enlightenment's urge to identify the trends of the time, encouraging those deemed positive, mitigating the negative, and methodically planning for the future.[12]

Even in his early youth, Franklin's life was a project of projects. Its elements were knowledge, self-improvement, improvement of society, and an understanding of the workings of the mind. In his teens, he plunged into Locke's hefty and dense *Essay concerning Human Understanding*. In later years, he "esteemed [it] the best Book of Logick in the World."[13]

Franklin was attuned to Locke's empirical rationality and wariness of religion. Thomas Kidd, a specialist on the founders' religious lives, has written, "Locke's packaging of rationalism and traditional Christian concepts made him irresistible to

Franklin, who was seeking an intellectual map with which to escape his Reformed Christian background. Already by his teen years, Franklin was pursuing a Christianity based on virtue and reason, not doctrine."[14]

Once Franklin learned to read the most demanding adult literature, he took the next step: teaching himself to compose his ideas with cogency, flair, and humor to promote his own ideas and critique—and emulate—those of others. He found a model in the London periodical *The Spectator*, cofounded by Joseph Addison. An influential figure in the English Enlightenment, Addison introduced his maiden issue thus: "It was said of Socrates that he brought philosophy down from heaven to inhabit among men; and I shall be ambitious to have it said of me that I have brought philosophy out of closets and libraries, schools and colleges, to dwell in clubs and assemblies, at tea tables and in coffee houses."[15]

Highbrow modern journalism—intellectual and political in content, rigorous in standards of reportage, accessible in style, laced with wit—was coming into its own in the mother country, and a boy in the colonies had found a job that would never be far from all of his talents and achievements.

———

Benjamin's first boss, mentor, and editor was his older brother, James, who founded the *New-England Courant*, one of the first American newspapers. His five years as an apprentice were tumultuous and left the brothers with lasting grudges. More than half a century after James's death in 1735, as Benjamin's long and illustrious life was coming to an end, his memoirs, unfinished and published posthumously, depicted James as a jealous, vindictive, even violent taskmaster. One sentence was particularly invidious: "I fancy his harsh and tyrannical Treatment of me might be a means of impressing me with that aversion to arbitrary power that has stuck to me through my whole life."[16] The insinuation could not be lost: James behaved toward his kid brother as King George III behaved toward his American subjects.

A number of Franklin's biographers have come to James's defense, not least because of Benjamin's silence about his brother's role as a pioneer and defender of a free press in the colonies.[17] James inaugurated the *Courant* with an invitation for "all Men, who have Leisure, Inclination and Ability, to speak their Minds with Freedom, Sense and Moderation, and their Pieces shall be welcome to a Place in my Paper."[18]

He was as good as his word. He printed protests, complaints, and unorthodox religious views that gave the colonial authorities fits, notably the Puritan patriarch Cotton Mather, who had intimidating clout in the community. Mather called the *Courant* a "Wickedness never parallel'd any where upon the Face of the Earth" and its contributors "the Hell-Fire Club." James pushed back: "To anathematize a Printer for publishing the different Opinions of Men is as injudicious as it is wicked." Mather had him jailed for his views.[19]

Whatever James's faults, he left a legacy he would never see: a free press for a free America. He died in 1735, leaving his wife to keep the business going. She eventually became the colony's official printer.[20]

The final rupture between the brothers had an ironic twist. When Benjamin, at seventeen, escaped from Boston, he was leaving James in the lurch, yet he was also following his brother's career path.

After short stints in New York and Philadelphia, Benjamin sailed to London to earn his journeyman printer credentials, much as James had at the same age.

———

When Franklin arrived in the center of the British world, good fortune struck. Not only did he find lodgings next to a bookshop, better still, he talked the proprietor into letting him borrow secondhand books at a pittance. A short time later, he got a job in a printing shop that published scholarly works, including those written by contemporary philosophers. Franklin was primed to make the most of living in the heart of the British Enlightenment. Deism was in its heyday in England, and that suited Franklin.[21] He was particularly taken with Anthony Collins, a flashy proponent of unvarnished deism. Before coming to London, the young American had read two of Collins's treatises attacking the "absurdities" of Christianity.[22]

Rather than just reading these competing discourses, he joined the fray by publishing one himself.

Soon an opportunity came his way. His employer, Samuel Palmer, had agreed to publish a new edition of *The Religion of Nature Delineated* by William Wollaston, a deist who had recently died. The apprentice, in his leather apron, composed, locked, and inked type on the press, then checked the proofs for typos. That was his job. But what he did next was not: he looked for flaws in the author's argument and found enough to promote himself, in his own eyes, as a budding philosopher. After hours in the shop, he labored over *A Dissertation on Liberty and Necessity, Pleasure, and Pain*, a rebuttal to Wollaston. He had prepared by studying a widely respected manual for the method, conventions, and jargon of the genre.[23] But his amateurism showed in garbles and contradictions, and he slipped into the breezy, satirical style of his columns for the *Courant*.[24]

As for the substance of his argument, he channeled Collins's sarcasm rather than Locke's skepticism. He began by presenting the reader with two propositions:

   i. There is said to be a *First Mover*, who is called god,
      Maker of the Universe.

   ii. He is said to be all-wise, all-good, all powerful.

He closed astringently:

Truth will be Truth tho' it sometimes prove mortifying and distasteful.[25]

In other words, a rational thinker should not expect divine grace or an afterlife.

While Franklin earned some praise, he took grief as well, including from Palmer, who called some of his conclusions "abominable" even if they showed "ingenuity." In his autobiography, Franklin downplayed his "little metaphysical piece" and wrote that printing it was "another erratum."[26]

Throughout his life, Franklin cultivated a triad of attributes that served him well: an unquenchable thirst for learning, self-confidence when plunging into the great issues of the day, and, at the same time, a degree of self-criticism when his curiosity and audacity got the better of him. When he was occupied by serious and sometimes dangerous matters, there was often a twinkle in his gimlet eye. He was a believer in the constant tension between progress and fallibility of the human enterprise. Franklin showed a cautious interest in Hobbes's works and Spinoza's ideas on God.[27] He wanted to judge for himself whether these controversial geniuses were, as many claimed, atheists or even satanists. He found them exemplars of sober rationalism, effective arguments, and bold concepts that were useful for political endeavors.[28]

As a rule, Franklin absented himself from religious debates, especially in public, but his insatiable curiosity sometimes got the better of him. In 1732, settled in Philadelphia, he gave a private lecture at the Junto Club, a gentlemen's discussion group. As a founding member, he felt comfortable among friends—not one of them a man of the cloth. Rather, they were practical-minded laymen: physician, mathematician, geographer, natural philosopher (scientist), botanist, chemist, and engineer. He titled his lecture "On the Providence of God in the Government of the World." After assaying various versions of God's existence and His interest in mortal affairs, triumphs, and follies, Franklin's conclusion was that humanity should not rely on God (call it Poor Richard's deism): God can, when it suits His infinite wisdom, share some of His infinite power with mortals in the form of free will. It was a compromise that probably satisfied neither the audience nor the lecturer.

Those who believed in God should "pray to him for his Favour and Protection"[29]—that might do some good and would do no harm—but when it came to getting things done, people "should have more dependence on *works*, than on *faith*."[30]

For the rest of his long life, Franklin would sidestep theology, since it was not a subject for rational discussion and cogitation. More than half a century after writing his only published philosophical tract, he wrote to a friend, "The great Uncertainty I found in Metaphysical Reasonings disgusted me, and I quitted that kind of Reading & Study, for others more satisfactory."[31]

———

Franklin felt on far more solid ground even when he was experimenting with electrical storms or charting the Gulf Stream as a faster route across the Atlantic. In his multiple and overlapping occupations—journalism, publishing, civic leadership—he was innovating those vocations. He was also looking for ways to improve people's lives, whether it be a better woodburning stove or a urinary catheter. His promotion of inoculation for smallpox enhanced Philadelphia's reputation as a mecca for medicinal care.[32]

In 1751 he published an article projecting population growth, in light of the immense unsettled land in America. He calculated that the colonies would overtake Britain itself within a century. Twenty years later, Adam Smith—whose pioneering work in economy was considered in that era to be a branch of moral philosophy—incorporated Franklin's calculations into his masterwork, *The Wealth of Nations*.[33] A star of the European Enlightenment was beholden to an autodidact from the transatlantic provinces of the empire.

In all his enthusiasms, whether vocational or recreational, Franklin followed a three-step method: first, follow your curiosity; second, understand what makes a thing work; and third, apply your resourcefulness to invent a new thing or to make the old one work better.

From that method, he derived the imperative for an open society. New ideas must be given a chance rather than squelched by orthodoxy or, worse, repressed by government. In 1731 he wrote a full-throated defense of freedom of speech and the press: "[While] the Opinions of Men are almost as various as their Faces, . . . printers are educated in the Belief, that when Men differ in Opinion, both Sides ought equally to have the Advantage of being heard by the Publick; and that when Truth and Error have fair Play, the former is always an overmatch for the latter."[34] He believed his fellow journalists and editors had two cardinal duties: to respect indisputable facts and to let their opinions be known.

———

Franklin spearheaded several institutions that helped in making independence and republicanism possible. At twenty-five, he founded America's first successful lending library in the English-

speaking world.[35] The Library Company of Philadelphia ener-
gized a movement that, over the next two decades, would spur
the establishment of the Redwood Library in Newport, Rhode
Island, and lending libraries in Charlestown, South Carolina,
and in New York.

Following Franklin's initiative, the Junto Club expanded its
membership and geographical scope under the new name of the
American Philosophical Society. Religious topics were rare,
while talks on botany, medicine, animal breeding, and other
hands-on matters thrived. Franklin wrote a prospectus for the
society emphasizing its dedication to "all philosophical Experiments that let Light into the Nature of Things, tend to increase
the Power of Man over Matter, and multiply the Conveniencies
or Pleasures of Life."[36]

Franklin was in the forefront in America's boom of higher
learning. British America had already made impressive strides in
higher education during the previous century, and more colleges
sprang up in the colonies in the 1700s. Franklin was prominent
in nurturing that movement.[37] In 1740, at the age of thirty-four,
he was key in creating a college that would educate both students from the working class and those from the higher ranks
of society. First called the Academy and Charitable School in
the Province of Pennsylvania, it later became the University of
Pennsylvania. Franklin was the inaugural president for six years
and a lifetime trustee.[38]

In 1775, as Franklin neared his eighth decade, the Continental Congress appointed this inveterate correspondent to be the first postmaster of the United States. That made him the official in charge of America's own Republic of Letters, integrating all thirteen states in the last months before the Declaration of Independence was signed. Before his service to the Revolution and what came after, he had already helped lay the foundation for a society ready for a new polity. His expansive pursuits constituted a lifelong experiment guided by logic and a vision of progress. His first occupation as a printer reinforced his respect for facts, as did his crusade to disseminate knowledge through schooling and a vigorous, responsible press. These convictions inspired younger founders, who would incorporate them into their own goals, methods, and ethics for leading the country.

Franklin's repute abroad, especially as a scientist, outshone any other American of his time. His droll wit and erudition mixed with a folksy persona (the beaver hat) dazzled European intellectuals, politicians, and courtiers. He received an honorary doctoral degree of civil law from Oxford in 1762—hence his title, Doctor—in addition to tributes from universities on the Continent.[39]

When independence came, Franklin, more than anyone else, had made the world ready to take America seriously.

5

Tea and Enmity

I am more and more grieved at the accounts of America.
Where this spirit will end is not to be said.

—*King George III*

Benjamin Franklin and George Washington were the most revered of the Revolutionary generation. When they reached the station of elders, their long experience as loyal colonists proved useful for their younger colleagues in making the case for America to break the bond of British rule.[1]

Their diverse paths converged in a prodigious victory. Franklin brought the blessings of the Enlightenment and modernity to America. Washington the soldier knew the necessity of war to achieve independence, but when victory came, he was adamant to keep peace with the powers of Europe lest they strangle the newborn republic. Washington's exposure to combat in his youth would gird him, two decades later, for the necessity of war and, then as president, of securing peace.

———

The immediate contention in the 1750s was whether the North American continent could accommodate two European empires. France claimed vast territory—Canada, the Great Lakes region, and a wide swath along the length of the Mississippi River valley—all inhabited by little more than seventy thousand French. British America was in the contrary position: a population of two million, hugging the mid-Atlantic seaboard. As more English settlers headed inland, they often expelled or decimated natives or forced them into servitude and engaged in altercations with the voyageurs, trappers, and settlers of New France.

British colonials had been harassing French outposts, and after several years, Franklin and others—including a growing war lobby in Westminster—pressed His Majesty's government to take on France full bore.[2] While the colonial hierarchy of Virginia was also eager to expand northward, King George II and his government were more cautious.

A dispute over the regulation of barge traffic in the Ohio River valley set off skirmishes that became pitched battles from Newfoundland to the southern colonies. Both sides had native warriors and scouts as allies, but the French, with their history of trading with the tribes rather than stealing their lands, had the upper hand.

The flashpoint came in 1754, with Washington, then twenty-two, unwittingly at the center. A newly minted lieutenant colonel in a Virginia regiment, he headed 160 troops into the Ohio Country (now western Pennsylvania) to reconnoiter French forces. Coming upon a smaller contingent of French soldiers, Washington and his men killed ten and took twenty-one prisoners. Soon after the bloodbath, Washington wrote, in a letter to his brother, Jack, "I can with truth assure you, I heard Bulletts whistle and believe me there was something charming in the sound."[3]

This gruesome but minor and accidental fracas spiraled into a major dispute in the chancelleries of London and Paris over who had fired the first shot.[4] Horace Walpole, a British historian and statesman, thought he knew the answer: "The volley fired by a young Virginian in the backwoods of America set the world on fire."[5]

———

The following year, Benjamin Franklin, in his capacity as postmaster, traveled to the disputed rough country to help with communications for the largest British expeditionary force ever deployed to America. Its mission, under the command of Major General Edward Braddock, was to eject the French from British-claimed territory.[6]

The outcome of what came to be known as the Battle of Monongahela was catastrophic. The British regulars panicked and retreated into the woods, only to find the enemy waiting to cut them down. Among the surviving colonials there was palpable shame, anger, and a germ of skepticism: Britannia might rule the waves, but she fell short in the interior of a continent. Franklin was acerbic in his autobiography: "This whole transaction gave us Americans the first suspicion that our exalted ideas of the prowess of British regulars had not been well founded."[7]

As for Washington, luck and pluck saved him. While no

doubt angry over the debacle, Washington took a constructive approach. In preparing for his military career, he had studied Humphrey Bland's *A Treatise of Military Discipline*, a field manual used by the British army. In the aftermath of the battle, he ordered the book for his subordinates so that they could glean lessons for their next encounter with the enemy.[8]

In 1756 the bloodletting in North America elided into the Seven Years' War, a global melee among major actors who divided into coalitions, costing as many as 1.5 million lives and spanning five regions around the earth.[9] The havoc ended in 1763 with the Treaty of Paris, hosted by the losers, who forfeited Canada and all territorial claims on mainland North America. This episode, in a land of largely uncharted forests and rivers, was a turning point. Habitants of the New World had goaded their rulers in the Old to play a catalytic role in history's first world war.[10]

While Britain's fortunes had taken a turn for the better, Washington's military career had not. In 1758 he was refused a commission by the British army, and he returned to Virginia, hung up his uniform, married, studied books on agriculture and animal husbandry, and managed a large plantation at Mount Vernon.

———

Although the Seven Years War came to an end, peacetime in America was not tranquil. Britain's new sovereign, George III, suspecting that his subjects in the colonies might have a nurturing ambition to be a continental power, set about tightening control of his imperial domain in North America.

Instead of honoring colonists' land grants wrested from France, King George transferred the lands beyond the Appalachian Mountains to natives, in hopes of subduing their antagonism. He also ordered his colonial governors to nullify laws enacted by the locals in the New World. Although the war was over, British military units remained. Most were located on the frontier, with some billeted in western New York.[11]

Britain's victory came with a heavy price. King George counted on his American subjects to help refill the coffers of the exchequer.

First, Parliament passed the America Revenue Act (also known as the Sugar Act) of 1764, which reduced the tax on molasses but tightened enforcement of its collection. In the following year, a stamp duty was levied on newspapers, pamphlets, legal documents, commercial bills, and even playing cards. It was the first time Britain had imposed an internal tax directly on Americans.

When Benjamin Franklin arrived in London as an agent of the colonies and learned of the passage of the Stamp Act, he knew that his mission would be contentious. Given his formidable debating skills and penchant for mocking English haughtiness, he was certain to make new enemies during his eleven-year stay in the motherland.

But he also had old friends, including several eminent figures of the British Enlightenment, who sympathized with the American cause. Among them were Edmund Burke, the erudite

Anglo-Irish leader of the Whigs, and Adam Smith. Both urged their government to temper its harsh mercantile and taxation policies, fearing the consequences for both sides if the colonies bolted.

When Franklin was grilled in the House of Commons about the protests back home, he was asked how the colonists would react if British soldiers were sent to enforce compliance. His response: "They will not find a rebellion; they may indeed make one."[12]

As news of the Stamp Act reached the American colonies, the Atlantic seaboard exploded with more protests, the most raucous in Boston.

No one was more seized by the issue than the twenty-nine-year-old John Adams.

———

For more than a decade, Adams had been honing his intellect, probing the lessons of history, and envisioning America's destiny. In the autumn of 1755, not long after graduating from Harvard, he wrote to a classmate summarizing a lesson from ancient history: The master states of the world started out as wildernesses inhabited by rustics, he wrote, only to be eclipsed by others who came later. "Immortal Rome" grew from "an insignificant village, inhabited only by a few abandoned Ruffins," until, over centuries, a distant, primitive province of that aging empire spawned the embryo of a new one, Britain, whose scope and power was now greater than Rome's.[13]

That was a mere prelude to Adams's prophecy: "Our People according to the exactest Computations, will in another Century, become more numerous than England itself. Should this be the Case, since we have (I may say) all the naval Stores of the Nation in our hands, it will be easy to obtain the mastery of the seas, and then the united force of all Europe, will not be able to subdue us. The only way to keep us from setting up for ourselves, is to disunite Us."[14]

Ten years later, Adams was newly married, practicing law, and writing political commentaries for local newspapers. When the Stamp Act hit, he was already working on a dissertation accusing the British government of abusing the colonies with at-avistic laws like those that had empowered the Anglican church and suppressed the lower ranks of English society:

> There seems to be a direct and formal design on foot, to enslave all America. This however must be done by degrees. The first step that is intended seems to be an entire subver-sion of the whole system of our Fathers, by an introduction of the cannon and feudal law, into America. The cannon and feudal systems tho' greatly mutilated in England, are not yet destroy'd. Like the temples and palaces, in which the great contrivers of them, once worship'd and inhabited, they exist in ruins; and much of the domineering spirit of them still remains.[15]

Only at the end of the polemic did Adams refer to the latest outrage, and his indictment went much further than taxation without representation: "It seems very manifest from the Stamp

Act itself, that a design is form'd to strip us in a great measure of the means of knowledge, by loading the Press, the Colleges, and even an Almanack and a News-Paper, with restraints and duties; and to introduce the inequalities and dependances of the feudal system, by taking from the poorer sort of people all their little subsistance, and conferring it on a set of stamp officers, distributors and their deputies."[16]

His righteous anger was laced with excitement that propitious and world-shaking events were on the horizon. As 1765 came to a close, Adams confided to his diary that the year had been the most exhilarating of his life:

> That enormous Engine, fabricated by the british Parliament, for battering down all the Rights and Liberties of America, I mean the Stamp Act, has raised and spread, thro the whole Continent, a Spirit that will be recorded to our Honour, with all future Generations. . . . Such and so universal has been the Resentment of the People, that every Man who has dared to speak in favour of the Stamps, or to soften the detestation in which they are held, how great soever his Abilities and Virtues had been esteemed before, or whatever his fortune, Connections and Influence had been, has been seen to sink into universal Contempt and Ignominy.[17]

According to Adams, the Stamp Act was a British stratagem limited not just to steal Americans' money but—far worse—to impoverish their means to acquire knowledge. Several passages in the dissertation were resonant of the works of the seventeenth-century European Enlightenment. "Let it be known," he wrote, "that British liberties are not the grants of princes or parliaments, but original rights, conditions of original contracts, coequal with prerogative and coeval with government.—That many of our rights are inherent and essential."[18] He also invoked two contemporaries to buttress his case: the renowned Scottish philosopher Lord Kames and the Genevan savant Jean-Jacques Rousseau.

Adams was a formative figure of the American Enlightenment, not least because he was ferocious in argument. The Enlightenment was an international and intergenerational debating club. Adams parted ways with enthusiasts of reason who scorned emotion and passion—two of Adams's signal traits. He instead sided with David Hume, who was skeptical of seventeenth-century rationalists, who put their faith in rigorous logic for understanding almost all phenomena. Hume accepted strict laws in nature, but not in human nature.

Decades later, Adams wrote, "Reason holds the helm, but passions are the gales."[19] Indeed, he steered many a difficult channel as sage and statesman, but his stormy temperament was discordant with his virtues and talents. He could be vain, snobbish, irascible, and self-destructive. After years of working and debating with him, Franklin remarked, "he means well for his Country, is always an honest Man, often a Wise One, but sometimes and in some things, absolutely out of his Sense."[20]

All the defects—Vesuvian temper, thin skin, acid tongue, black brooding, and flights of fancy—are there in the testimonies of those who knew Adams, but so are affection, admiration, and awe of his scope and depth. Even Franklin's jibe came after three compliments.

And there was at least one more asset that Franklin failed to note: Adams was a realist in an age of idealism. "The perfectibility of man is only human and terrestrial perfectibility," he wrote. "Cold will still freeze, and fire will never cease to burn; disease and vice will continue to disorder, and death to terrify mankind." He urged that "sobriety" was essential for the truly enlightened mind, lest pretty lights obscure the truth and reality themselves.[21]

The young Thomas Jefferson, however, was intoxicated with the Enlightenment. At the age of sixteen, he came under the thrall of William Small, a professor at the College of William and Mary. He was also a child of the Scottish Enlightenment that was flourishing in the eighteenth century. The universities—St. Andrews, Glasgow, Edinburgh, and Aberdeen (Small's alma mater)— were closing in on the ranks of Oxbridge.

The Scots were forthright and inclined to make their views understandable to laymen. Francis Hutcheson, who taught moral philosophy at Glasgow, was the first of the renowned Scottish freethinkers, and his writings were known and respected in the British colonies by the time Jefferson came under Small's wing. It was there that the teenager was introduced to a philosopher who had moved well beyond Locke's reforms and strictures for a truly liberal government. He was adamantly opposed to hereditary monarchy and made the case for "pure democracy," a concept that would loom large in Jefferson's later life.[22] Joseph

Ellis notes that "Jefferson's belief in the natural equality of man derived primarily from Hutcheson's doctrine of the 'moral sense,' a faculty inherent in all human beings that no mere government could violate."[23]

Jefferson had recently lost his father and, for the rest of his life, remembered the twenty-five-year-old Small as a paternal surrogate.[24] Half a century later, Jefferson credited him with being the person who "probably fixed the destinies of my life . . . a man profound in most of the useful branches of science, with a happy talent of communication, correct and gentlemanly manners, and an enlarged and liberal mind."[25]

More important, Small helped Jefferson make the most of his keen and venturous intellect in multiple fields of inquiry: science, ethics, rhetoric, and belles lettres. Small's pupil mastered Greek, Latin, Italian, Spanish, and French. The last of these would serve him in reading the works of *les Lumières* in the original.[26] Jefferson excelled in all those subjects, except in theology, no doubt because of Small's influence. As the only layman among the teachers in the college, Small did not spare his colleagues his low opinion of mainstream Christianity, dismissing miracles, angels, virgin birth, and resurrection as superstitions.[27] He inculcated a lifelong skepticism of religion in his prize pupil.

In 1765, shortly after graduating and studying the law, Jefferson stood in a corridor outside a packed hall of the Virginia House of Burgesses to hear the debate about the Stamp Act in which Patrick Henry called King George "a Caesar" who deserved "his Brutus."[28]

The following year, while balancing his private law practice and interest in politics, Jefferson set forth on a solo journey on horseback up the seaboard—the first time he had left his "country," Virginia.[29] After crossing into Maryland, he headed for Annapolis, the seat of the colonial assembly, arriving at a moment of local elation. Word had just arrived that Parliament had repealed the Stamp Act. The news itself was exhilarating, but so was the spectacle of Marylanders' patriotic spirit mirroring his own.

Jefferson rode on to Philadelphia to be inoculated against smallpox (largely thanks to Benjamin Franklin), then headed for New York, where he watched soldiers from the local British garrison skirmish with the crowds of locals and Sons of Liberty, a clandestine organization active throughout the colonies.

The young Virginian returned to his home with a sense that he and the colony were part of something vast and expanding, bound together by similar cultures and aspirations, dynamism in society, breakthroughs in science and medicine, and a shared cause.[30] Patrick Henry, in his grandiloquent style, announced, "The Distinctions between Virginians, Pensylvanians [sic], New Yorkers and New Englanders, are no more. I am not a Virginian, but an American."[31]

———

The jubilation did not last long. Parliament's repeal of the Stamp Act was not meant to placate the colonists—far from it. British merchants were losing business. Politicians at Westminster sent a clear message on that score, asserting the British government's power to legislate for the colonies "in all cases whatsoever."[32]

Subsequent British provocations were certain, and one came the next year. Charles Townshend, the chancellor of the exchequer, proposed taxes on lead, paper, paint, glass—and tea. The soothing beverage relished by both Londoners and Bostonians was about to tear them apart. Predictably, the colonists took to the streets. His Majesty's prime minister, Lord North, dispatched two regiments to enforce the tax laws in Massachusetts.

————

Many Britons in high places were slow to understand what was happening in the colonies and how fast resistance was gathering momentum. In January 1774, they experienced a rude awakening. Reports had just reached London that the Massachusetts branch of the Sons of Liberty had boarded three British merchant ships anchored in Boston Harbor and dumped overboard 342 chests filled with forty-five tons of tea.

Meanwhile, Benjamin Franklin was back in London, the city that exhilarated him during his youth. Now he was representing the colonies in their objections to British government while hoping for a peaceful resolution.

Such an outcome seemed unlikely, as Parliament erupted over the news from Boston. Franklin took the brunt of their rage. Summoned to the Westminster chamber known as the Cockpit, he stood stoically while the members shouted, hurled insults, and treated him like a villain who had committed a capital crime.

The biographer H. W. Brands sums up the ordeal and its consequences: "Revolutions are not made in a morning, nor empires lost in a day. But Britain did itself more damage in those two hours than anyone present imagined. By alienating Franklin, the British government showed itself doubly inept: for making an enemy of a friend, and for doing so of the ablest and most respected American alive. At a moment when independence was hardly dreamed of in America, Franklin understood that to independence America must come."[33]

So, too, did many of his compatriots back home. Although no blood was shed during the serious hijinks in Boston, the British closed the harbor and imposed retaliatory measures against Massachusetts. Eleven other colonies (Georgia failed to send a delegation) fell in to organize resistance against British retaliations. Militant patriots formed shadow governments throughout the colonies, mustering militias, and marshaling stocks of munitions. They were already calling themselves patriots of a republic that was still a dream—and a project.

6

Red Sky at Morning

The battle of Lexington on the 19th of April changed the
instruments of warfare from the pen to the sword.

—*John Adams*

The man who would be eulogized as "first in war, first in peace, and first in the hearts of his countrymen" considered himself a proper Englishman until the age of forty-three.[1] His metamorphosis began when Britain's barrage of revenue policies hit Virginia hard, infuriating planters, businessmen, and land speculators, all hoping for a peace dividend following the French and Indian War.[2] But it was not until the winter of 1768–1769, when Parliament threatened to arrest the ringleaders of the growing resistance and bring them to England to be tried for treason, that George Washington countenanced active protest, although not yet revolution.

He supported an embargo of British goods, explaining his position in a letter to George Mason, a friend and Virginia politician who would be a major figure in debates, nation building, and governing:

At a time when our lordly Masters in Great Britain will be satisfied with nothing less than the deprivation of American freedom, it seems highly necessary that something shou'd be done to avert the stroke and maintain the liberty which we have derived from our Ancestors; but the manner of doing it to answer the purpose effectually is the point in question.

That no man shou'd scruple, or hesitate a moment to use a—ms in defence of so valuable a blessing, on which all the good and evil of life depends; is clearly my opinion; Yet A—ms I wou'd beg leave to add, should be the last resource; the de[r]nier resort. Addresses to the Throne, and remonstrances to parliament, we have already, it is said, proved the inefficacy of; how far then their attention to our rights & priviledges is to be awakened or alarmed by starving their Trade & manufactures, remains to be tryed.[3]

Here was a loyal Briton, well past the midpoint of his life—a professional soldier for whom war was not a glorious abstraction—invoking Enlightenment ideals of freedom and liberty, suggesting he was now being pulled in two directions.

———

By the fall of 1774, after the British navy blockaded Boston Harbor, Washington agreed to attend the First Continental Congress in Philadelphia. Parliament had slapped a new battery of reprisals to punish Massachusetts and warn other colonies. London called the set of measures the Coercive Acts; the colonials renamed them the Intolerable Acts. Once again, Great Britain's heavy-handed approach had backfired. Congress convened to decide the next steps, with some delegations (notably

Pennsylvania and New York) pushing for compromise while others favored revolution.

Shortly after his arrival with the Virginia delegation, Washington met John Adams in a pub, where they struck up a conversation.[4] It was the first encounter between the future first and second presidents. Their ensuing partnership would have its strains—Washington was taciturn, Adams voluble—but they shared basic convictions. One was a crucial ideal in their times and ours: Americans' right to choose any religion or none. Both embraced the Enlightenment principle that a person's spiritual belief was no one else's business.

Adams referred to himself as a "church going animal," a member of the Congregational church, who spent many Sundays sampling Philadelphia's diverse houses of worship: Anglican, Methodist, Baptist, Presbyterian, Quaker, and German Moravian. He sometimes attended three services in a day, comparing and grading the services and preachers.[5]

Washington joined him on one of these Sabbath outings to observe a mass at St. Mary's Catholic Church. The two visitors—one a short, portly, loquacious Boston lawyer, the other tall, ramrod-straight, reserved Virginian—must have aroused a curiosity among the parishioners.[6] Adams wrote to his wife, "The Musick consisting of an organ, and a Choir of singers, went all the Afternoon, excepting sermon Time, and the Assembly chanted—most sweetly and exquisitely. Here is every Thing which can lay hold of the Eye, Ear, and Imagination. Every Thing which can charm and bewitch the simple and ignorant. I wonder how Luther ever broke the spell."[7]

Adams and Washington, neither simple nor ignorant, were breaking yet another spell of Britannia in all her helmeted majesty. Unlike the protectors of the Church of England, the two Americans had no interest in suppressing "popery." Now that they were standing up to the British Empire, they certainly had no fear of the Holy Roman Empire, then in its dotage.

———

As delegates waited for other out-of-towners to arrive for the Congress, they had a wide choice of books at their lodgings, compliments of Benjamin Franklin's Library Company. Among those works was *The Spirit of the Law*, by Montesquieu, who was one of the most influential of *les Lumières* and who popularized the word *despotisme*. Like Locke, Montesquieu advocated for the separation of powers, along with strong procedural due process—the right to a fair trial, presumption of innocence, and proportionality in severity of punishment—abetted by freedom of thought, speech, and assembly. Montesquieu also promoted free trade, not just for economic efficiencies but as a curb on a bellicosity among nations: "Wherever there is commerce, there we meet with agreeable manners."[8]

———

While Congress was underway, Thomas Jefferson was in Virginia working on a tract called "A Summary View of the Rights of British America." (The title made clear that some colonials, while increasingly impatient, were prepared to reconcile with the Crown if Parliament would concede to or at least compromise on a growing list of demands.) In closing, Jefferson addressed King George directly, respectfully but candidly (one of his favorite words):

> That these are our grievances which we have thus laid before his majesty with that freedom of language and sentiment which becomes a free people, claiming their rights as derived from the laws of nature, and not as the gift of their chief magistrate. . . . Open your breast Sire, to liberal and expanded thought. Let not the name of George the third be a blot in the page of history. . . . The whole art of government consists in the art of being honest.[9]

Jefferson's offering of an olive branch elevated him in the eyes of those Virginians who wanted to avoid separation. Washington, who was among them, distributed copies of "Mr. Jefferson's Bill of Rights" to his friends, making it clear that war should be averted. No "thinking man in all North America"[10] would disagree.

———

By the following spring Washington had accepted that the undesirable must bend to the inevitable. On April 16, 1775, the Royal Navy sloop *Falcon* arrived in Boston harbor carrying General Thomas Gage, with orders to lay the ground to reestablish British control and "arrest and imprison the principal actors and abettors in the Provincial Congress (whose proceedings appear in every light to be acts of treason and rebellion)."[11] Gage's first action was to secure two bridges over the Concord River. Loyalist spies had reported that there would be little opposition other than "parties of bushmen."[12]

Five days later, British and American soldiers first engaged on the Lexington Green, then at Concord. The "bushmen"— Minute Men (armed farmers)—attacked the redcoats on their way to Concord and as they tried orderly to march in retreat to the safety of Boston. As Rick Atkinson relates in *The British Are Coming,* "The butcher's bill was grim indeed. British casualties totaled 273, nearly 15 percent of the total force that marched into Middlesex on April 19; of those, 73 men were killed or would die of their wounds. American casualties numbered 95, over half of them—49—dead."[13]

Great Britain had found its Rubicon, and so had America.

———

In June 1775, when the Second Continental Congress convened, with all thirteen colonies represented, Adams navigated Washington's candidacy for command of the Continental Army. He had a record for bravery during the French and Indian War, political experience starting in the Virginia House of Burgesses, a reputation for probity, and a commanding bearing. While often laconic, he was judicious and authoritative when he spoke, and—a clincher—he was a veteran warrior and politician from the most populous, largest, and wealthiest of the colonies.

The vote was unanimous. The newly promoted general's immediate challenge was to knit a collage of militias into a single, coordinated force, just as he would, in due course, lead a united nation.[14]

On his way from Philadelphia to Massachusetts to take up his duties in a region that was already at war, Washington gave a speech to the New York Provincial Congress. "When we assume the soldier," he said, "we did not lay aside the citizen."[15] Dispensing with the royal "we," he took up the republican one, foreshadowing "We the People" when the Constitution was ratified a dozen years later. For the next eight years, roughly a quarter of a million citizen-soldiers would be under his command, and at least twenty-five thousand would lay down their lives for their country, the greatest proportion of the population to die in any conflict other than the Civil War.[16]

The carnage would have been worse if Washington had not dealt with a silent and invisible peril. As a nineteen-year-old, he had visited Barbados. This was the only journey in his life that took him from the American mainland. He was there long enough to contract smallpox and returned to Virginia with minor but permanent scarring and a lifelong respect for medical science.

Nearly a quarter-century later, when Washington was mustering the Continental Army, he immediately dealt with an outbreak of the disease. Among his first decrees in the summer of 1775 was to quarantine anyone with symptoms. He knew that the virus could be more lethal than "the Sword of the Enemy."[17] Later in the war, he ordered new recruits to be inoculated as part of their enlistment.

Washington's actions were critical. Many British and German soldiers coming from Europe, where the disease was widespread, were now occupiers. Hence, they had already been exposed to the virus and were immune, while the Americans, both civilians and soldiers, would not have that advantage.[18]

———

In May 1775, while combat raged in the North, Thomas Jefferson, on his hill in the Blue Ridge Mountains, wrote two letters to intimates. One looked back with nostalgia and affection, the other was thinly threatening.

The first was to William Small, Jefferson's cherished teacher. Not long after Jefferson graduated from William and Mary, Small was refused the presidency of the college. He gave up teaching, returned to England, and became a doctor in Birmingham.

Accompanying the letter were three dozen bottles of Madeira, aged for eight years in Jefferson's Monticello cellar. Now that the American and British armies were spilling blood, he wanted to assure Small that nothing in the world would rupture their relationship, not even a break between Britain and the colonies.

His letter regretted "the unhappy news of an action of considerable magnitude between the king's troops and our brethren of Boston. . . . That such an action has happened is undoubted, tho' perhaps the circumstances may not yet have reached us with truth. This accident has cut off our last hopes of reconciliation, and a phrenzy of revenge seems to have seized all ranks of people."[19]

Small would never receive the gift or letter. He had contracted malaria in Virginia a decade earlier and succumbed at the age of forty, three months before his protégé reached out to him.[20]

A committed and influential American child of the Enlightenment had lost his intellectual mentor, one who had led Jefferson to forsake allegiance to Britain and commit to a union of sovereign states.

————

The second letter was to a Loyalist cousin, John Randolph, who was on his way to London. Jefferson's tone was more sorrowful than angry, but the message was stark:

> I hope the returning wisdom of Great Britain will e'er long put an end to this unnatural contest. . . . My first wish is a restoration of our just rights; my second a return of the happy period when, consistently with duty, I may withdraw myself totally from the public stage and pass the rest of my days in domestic ease and tranquillity, banishing every desire of afterwards even hearing what passes in the world. . . . But this was before blood was spilt. I cannot affirm, but have reason to think, these terms [compromises] would not now be accepted.[21]

He warned that if the spiral continued on its course, the "parent country" would find itself at war not just with its erstwhile colonies but with major powers that would come to America's aid: "If indeed Great Britain, disjoined from her colonies, be a match for the most potent nations of Europe with the colonies thrown into their scale, they may go on securely. But if they are not assured of this, it would be certainly unwise, by trying the event of another campaign, to risque our accepting a foreign aid which perhaps may not be obtainable but on a condition of everlasting avulsion from Great Britain."

He concluded with an uncharacteristic, brutal blow: "I am one of those too who rather than submit to the right of legislating for us assumed by the British parliament, and which late experience has shewn they will so cruelly exercise, would lend my hand to sink the whole island in the ocean."

While Washington was trying to stem wave after wave of British frigates crammed with redcoats and Hessian auxiliaries in New England, his fellow founders, mostly civilians, were looking ahead to sending their imperial armies back across the sea. To achieve that, they would need to proclaim their motives and resolve to their foes, their countrymen, and their world.

7

Indictments and Ideals

Well, if they cannot be happy under my government,
I hope they may not change it for the worse.

—*King George III*

Early in 1776, while John Adams was making his bleak winter journey of more than three hundred miles from Boston to Philadelphia on horseback, he was composing in his head, then jotting down in his diary when rested, a to-do list to use when going to work with his colleagues. A statement of purpose was paramount. Adams was unyielding on two points: "Government to be assumed by every colony" (that is, state government), and a "Declaration of Independency" (that is, no submission to British rule).[1] Rick Atkinson describes that document as "the proclamation intended to transform a squalid family brawl into a cause as ambitious and righteous as any in human history."[2]

Adams was well suited to the role of principal drafter. He was a disciplined, persuasive, and experienced lawyer. However, despite his attributes to indict the British king, the onus—and the renown—fell to Thomas Jefferson in one of the most consequential divorces in history.

And so once again, the Virginia factor was decisive: Jefferson, just thirty-three but a respected wordsmith, would put quill to parchment for the first iteration.[3]

The document had the mark of Jefferson's keen intellect and stylistic elegance and displayed a fine-tuned duality encompassing idealism and realism, bold ideas and pragmatism. He drew on his reading of the British and French Enlightenments, the ancient Greeks, and the republican Romans.

———

Nearly half a century later, with barely a year to live, Jefferson was asked what the greatest accomplishment of the Declaration of Independence had been. His answer:

> When forced, therefore, to resort to arms for redress, an appeal to the tribunal of the world was deemed proper for our justification. This was the object of the Declaration of Independence. Not to find out new principles, or new arguments, never before thought of, not merely to say things which had never been said before; but to place before mankind the common sense of the subject, in terms so plain and firm, as to command their assent, and to justify ourselves in the independent stand we are compelled to take. Neither aiming at originality of principle or sentiment, nor yet copied from any particular and previous writing, it was intended to be an expression of the American mind, and to give to that expression the proper tone and spirit called for by the occasion. All its authority rests then on the harmonizing sentiments of the day, whether expressed in conversations, in

letters, printed essays, or in the elementary books of public right, as Aristotle, Cicero, Locke, Sidney, etc.[4]

This reflection, a blend of feigned modesty and authentic audacity, was very much a Jeffersonian trait. He gave credit to the harbingers of previous centuries while congratulating the founders, including himself, who took the ideas of the past and molded them into political reality, something new under the sun.

Jefferson read capaciously and eclectically, with a critical eye. For his assignment in Philadelphia, John Locke's works were exemplary, largely because they encompassed the life of the mind and the life of society. Jefferson read Locke's *Second Treatise on Government* at least three times.[5] Locke propounded the founder's three most salient tenets: human beings are entitled to basic and equal rights, precisely because they are human; governments derive their legitimacy from the consent of the governed; and governments that fail to respect and protect the people's rights forfeit their right to govern.

————

Just as Jefferson had claimed the prerogative of "editing" Locke, a committee—principally Franklin and Adams—edited Jefferson. (Roger Sherman of Connecticut and Robert Livingston of New York, also on the committee, had less input than the formidable three.)[6] Scholars give Jefferson credit for the opening, which obliged him to thread the needle on the issue of religion to enable the devout and the skeptical to come together on the language. The first thirty-three words laid the premise that humanity's fortune is in its own hands: "When in the Course of human events it becomes necessary for one people to dissolve the political bands which have connected them with another and to assume among the powers of the earth. . . ." Only after emphasizing human agency did he refer to divine approval, continuing, "the separate and equal station to which the Laws of Nature and of Nature's God entitle them, a decent respect to the opinions of mankind requires that they should declare the causes which impel them to the separation."[7]

Jefferson knew that delegates conventional in their religious beliefs would want God recognized in the preamble. Adams definitely was in that category and, no doubt, was keeping an eye on Jefferson and Franklin, his colleagues of dubious piety.

Even so, instead of evoking the Almighty in His solitary splendor, Jefferson affiliated God with nature's laws, a reference that preceded God by name, suggesting perhaps that God is part of nature's realm, rather than the other way around. If so, Jefferson was freeing the new government to make laws that conform with those of nature, and the taproot of equality and individual rights.[8]

So much for God in the document, in spite of some delegates' insistence on referring to "the Supreme Judge of the world" and "Divine Providence" in the final paragraph.

Numerous scholars believe that Jefferson gave a nod to the seventeenth-century freethinkers who doubted the existence of a supreme being, a lord of the universe guiding human affairs and attending to human souls. Danielle Allen believes that "Jefferson drafted the Declaration carefully so that neither the deist nor the Christian conception of God is presupposed."[9]

"Nature's God" was suggestive of Locke, Hobbes, Hutcheson, and Spinoza, even if few would dare to mention him.[10] Whether Jefferson was giving a wink to the last of this quartet is part of long-running conjecture that will probably remain just that. His library at Monticello contained three of Spinoza's works—*Theologico-Political Treatise, Opera posthuman,* and *A Treatise Partly Theological, and Partly Political*—that were rarely read in the eighteenth century.[11] Jefferson often said that he did not just collect books—he read them. A letter that he wrote to John Adams late in life contained tantalizing reference to "disciples" of Spinoza and other philosophers who had "naturalistic" ideas about God.[12]

In the second sentence of his early draft, Jefferson conflated several Lockean passages from *The Second Treatise*: "We hold these truths to be sacred & undeniable; that all men are created equal & independant, that from that equal creation they derive rights inherent & inalienable, among which are the preservation of life, & liberty, & the pursuit of happiness."[13]

Delegates were already looking over Jefferson's shoulder. Rather than "all men are created equal and independent," he gave in to pious colleagues who wanted the Creator Himself to be named, not just creation as a natural phenomenon.

From another perspective, Franklin—a professional editor— may have shortened the beginning of the second sentence to give it more punch and make it more compatible with the logic and lexicon of the Enlightenment. As America's pragmatist in chief, he may have deleted "sacred" because of its intimation that the creation of an independent republic required divine approval and intervention. Like Jefferson, Franklin wanted the focus to be on individual rights, sovereignty, freedom of thought, and projects that would change the world. Adams might have objected, but if so, he was outvoted by his crypto-deist colleagues.

Franklin probably also dropped "undeniable," which smacked of dogma, and substituted "self-evident." Forensically, it was a preemptive check on dissent, and philosophically, an assertion that requires no further evidence of proof, since existence proves itself.

With those two changes, Isaacson notes, "Franklin's edit turned [the sentence] . . . into an assertion of rationality."[14] Freethinkers through the ages have believed that rationality is what renders humans human. A defining theme of the Enlightenment was that all individuals are born freethinkers, or should be, and certainly should be allowed to be.

The founders were not just unshackling themselves from a monarchy, nor solely creating a government that would protect the rights of the people. Instead, they were conveying to citizens not just their right but their responsibility to choose their government.

A crucial and very long subordinate clause amplified the second paragraph's reference to the "inalienable rights" of life, liberty, and the pursuit of happiness: "That to secure these rights, Governments are instituted among Men, deriving their just powers from the consent of the governed, —That whenever any Form of Government becomes destructive of these ends, it is the Right of the People to alter or to abolish it, and to institute new Government, laying its foundation on such principles and organizing its powers in such form, as to them shall seem most likely to effect their Safety and Happiness."[15]

Next came a sentence on the necessity of separation from Britain: "Prudence, indeed, will dictate that Governments long established should not be changed for light and transient causes; and accordingly all experience hath shewn, that mankind are more disposed to suffer, while evils are sufferable, than to right themselves by abolishing the forms to which they are accustomed."

And then, following a long list of profound offenses suffered at the hands of the Crown, came the statement, "A Prince whose character is thus marked by every act which may define a Tyrant, is unfit to be the ruler of a free people."

———

In these magisterial passages, Jefferson was adhering to the rules defining the age of reason, but with an unabashed utopian persuasion. "Though indebted to Locke," Joseph Ellis writes, "Jefferson's political vision was more radical than liberal, driven as it was by a youthful romanticism unwilling to negotiate its high standards with an imperfect world."[16]

Jefferson had constructed a syllogism of three propositions: all human beings come into this world equal under the laws of nature; therefore every human being has a right to life, liberty, and the pursuit of happiness; finally, if a government imposes repressive laws on them, the people have the right to revolt and seek independence.[17]

The third principle was, effectively, a declaration of war. The enemy of freedom is tyranny. Unlike his direct address to George III in "A Summary View of the Rights of British America" two years earlier, here Jefferson dropped the courtesies. Now he was in prosecutorial as well as philosophical mode: "Such has been the patient sufferance of these Colonies; and such is now the necessity which constrains them to alter their former Systems of Government. The history of the present King of Great Britain is a history of repeated injuries and usurpations, all having in direct object the establishment of an absolute Tyranny over these States. To prove this, let Facts be submitted to a candid world."

———

Jefferson's logic chain begged for a fourth link that was problematic and inescapably implicit in the first two: the equality and rights of "man." The word itself implies not just all men of all races, but the other half of humanity. In practice, however, only white men qualified.

The latter issue—the roles and rights of women—seemed to have received virtually no mention in the Pennsylvania State House. Two months earlier, Adams had received a letter with a piece of Abigail's mind on the subject:

> I long to hear that you have declared an independancy—and
> by the way in the new Code of Laws which I suppose it will

be necessary for you to make I desire you would Remember the Ladies, and be more generous and favourable to them than your ancestors. Do not put such unlimited power into the hands of the Husbands. Remember all Men would be tyrants if they could. If perticuliar care and attention is not paid to the Laidies we are determined to foment a Rebelion, and will not hold ourselves bound by any Laws in which we have no voice, or Representation.

That your Sex are Naturally Tyrannical is a Truth so thoroughly established as to admit of no dispute, but such of you as wish to be happy willingly give up the harsh title of Master for the more tender and endearing one of Friend. Why then, not put it out of the power of the vicious and the Lawless to use us with cruelty and indignity with impunity.[18]

Adams blew her off:

As to your extraordinary Code of Laws, I cannot but laugh. We have been told that our Struggle has loosened the bands of Government every where. That Children and Apprentices were disobedient—that schools and Colledges were grown turbulent—that Indians slighted their Guardians and Negroes grew insolent to their Masters. But your Letter was the first Intimation that another Tribe more numerous and powerfull than all the rest were grown discontented.—This is rather too coarse a Compliment but you are so saucy, I wont blot it out.

Depend upon it, We know better than to repeal our Masculine systems. Altho they are in full Force, you know they are little more than Theory. We dare not exert our Power in its full Latitude. We are obliged to go fair, and softly, and in Practice you know We are the subjects. We have only the Name of Masters, and rather than give up this, which would compleatly subject Us to the Despotism of the Peticoat, I hope General Washington, and all our brave Heroes would fight.[19]

The "Ladies," a tribe? One can imagine Abigail rolling her eyes.[20]

———

As for slavery, it was already a lethal poison in the American bloodstream. The Declaration had two goals: trumpeting admirable ideals that would come with independence and castigating Great Britain for all evils. Britain was indeed initially to blame, going back to 1619 at Jamestown. But now that the continental colonies were set on transforming themselves as self-governing states, the onus was on them to live up to the righteous, liberal, and enlightened pronouncement that their delegates would soon be signing.

In fact, as the split widened between Britain and the colonies on the American mainland, another opened with the British-ruled islands in the West Indies. Those white islanders were not about to join the cause of independence, largely because they needed British soldiers to protect them from decades of slave revolts.

During the years of rising tensions, the British government played the slavery card against the increasingly rebellious colonials. Lord North commissioned Samuel Johnson—an outspoken abolitionist—to respond to the complaints coming from Philadelphia: "How is it that we hear the loudest yelps for liberty among the drivers of negroes?"

The founders had already heard the charge of hypocrisy from one of their own, Benjamin Rush, a physician who studied at the University of Edinburgh in the heyday of the Scottish Enlightenment: "Where is the difference between the British Senator who attempts to enslave his fellow subjects, in America, by imposing Taxes upon them contrary to Law and Justice; and the American Patriot who reduces his African Brethren to Slavery, contrary to Justice and Humanity?"[21]

It was an important question, to which the delegates had no satisfactory answer. There were those who believed that God made man in two forms, master and slave, and even color-coded them so there would be no question who dominated the other. There were some who abominated the practice but said little and did nothing; some who heroically and futilely demanded abolition and emancipation; and others who believed slavery would simply die out naturally, without government action. (Those in the last category forgot the importance of human agency.) Some claimed to be abolitionists in theory but were not in practice, while others had never owned slaves and genuinely detested the institution.

As for Thomas Jefferson, he was at his most sphinx-like in his draft of the Declaration:

He [King George] has waged cruel war against human nature itself, violating its most sacred rights of life & liberty in the persons of a distant people who never offended him, captivating & carrying them into slavery in another hemisphere, or to incur miserable death in their transportation thither. this piratical warfare, the opprobrium of infidel powers, is the warfare of the Christian king of Great Britain. determined to keep open a market where men should be bought & sold, he has prostituted his negative for suppressing every legislative attempt to prohibit or to restrain this execrable commerce: and that this assemblage of horrors might want no fact of distinguished die, he is now exciting those very people to rise in arms among us, and to purchase that liberty of which he has deprived them, & murdering the people upon whom he also obtruded them; thus paying off former crimes committed against the liberties of one people, with crimes which he urges them to commit against the lives of another.[22]

Those 168 words formed the most ardent, bloodcurdling passage in his draft. Since he was blaming King George for every other crime on the docket, he might as well add this one. But the passage begged for recognition of American culpability for American bondage. In any event, Jefferson's colleagues excised the passage in toto, in many cases because they did not want the document to mention slavery.

The resistant delegates were not limited to southern slaveholders. There were northerners whose constituents were profiting from the shipyards supplying vessels for the journey between the West Coast of Africa and the East Coast of the Americas. The slaveowners among them were willing buyers and sellers in the market of human beings. While Jefferson castigated the king of Britain, some two hundred slaves were working at Monticello.[23]

The Declaration was a consensus document, not a dictate enforced by an existing state. Rather, it was backed by the eloquence of the authors but also by the receptivity of their audience. The key words were aspirational, but the drafters had to take account of the disparate traditions, mores, and beliefs in the hall. The representatives of the former thirteen colonies asserted that the "one people" of "the thirteen united States of America" were dissolving their ties with Britain, though many of their constituents were still loyal to the Crown. The most important word in the document was "unanimous." An impasse would ensure defeat in the war already raging. Without unanimity in the hall, America would be stillborn.

Therein was the crux that was, purposely, not addressed. Jefferson's notes on the debate suggest that he considered siding with "Northern brethren [who] also I believe felt a little tender under those censures" coming from the southern delegates. Yet he joined the majority, consisting of representatives from the cotton kingdom and others who did not want to risk blowing up the Congress.[24]

Rush and his fellow abolitionists feared that the Declaration's implicit condoning of slavery would tarnish the nation's moral reputation and fester as the years went by.[25] They were right, but first, the signers and their constituents had to fight against Britain, and that meant a united America. Fighting slavery would have to wait for another day and another war.

8

A World Awaiting

This is the greatest thing in North America: Europe
is the greatest thing in North America!

—*Delmore Schwartz*

As the delegates filed out of the Pennsylvania State House, an initial wave of British troops had come ashore on Staten Island. The contingent would swell to more than thirty thousand within the following weeks.

For the Americans, there would be no going back, no quasi-peace. The founders knew that their very lives were at stake. Benjamin Harrison of Virginia—the father of William Henry Harrison, the ninth president, and great-grandfather of Benjamin Harrison, the twenty-third—came up with a quip that became famous. Bantering with his lean, diminutive colleague, Elbridge Gerry of Massachusetts, the corpulent, six-foot-four Harrison joked that his girth would make his hanging quick, while Gerry would "dance in the air an hour or two before you are dead."[1]

As gallows humor was making its rounds in Philadelphia, one can only imagine the mood of the motley soldiers readying to go into battle with the British behemoth that had experience in conquering far-off lands and stamping out insurrections. John Hancock, the president of the Continental Congress, sent a copy of the Declaration to George Washington's headquarters in New

York with a directive that the brigade majors should read it aloud to their troops in hopes of steeling their courage and pride in their goal.[2]

As the British saw it, any subject of the Crown who bore arms against the king's soldiers was a traitor. The colonials turned rebels would expect the gamut of miseries, chaos, and evils of war: fatal blunders, cruelty, starvation rations, disease, wanton destruction, vengeance, executions, mutinies, prison ships, and, above all, the slaughter of pitched battles.

Yet the revolutionaries had an advantage: They were fighting and spilling their blood on their own soil. Moreover, Britain in the eighteenth century was a superpower that incited jealousy and fear among other European governments and populaces. In June 1776, Benjamin Franklin used a historical event to buttress Washington's faith in the Patriot cause: "I see in it a Detail of the mighty Force we are [threatened] with; which however I think it is not certain will ever arrive; and I see more certainly the Ruin of Britain if she persists in such expensive distant Expeditions, which will probably prove more disastrous to her than anciently her Wars in the Holy Land."[3]

Thomas Jefferson had a conviction that an independent America would not only earn respect abroad; he foresaw that the modern republic would find imitators. Garry Wills, whose several books on the birth of the United States emphasize the stimulus of the Enlightenment, suggests that "Jefferson surely wanted to impress others with the spectacle of American virtues; and that was the way to motivate others toward virtue in [the Scottish philosopher Francis] Hutcheson's system," a liberal international order.[4]

The historian David Armitage writes that the Declaration was "addressed as much to the world at large as to the population of the American colonies."[5] John Adams, too, claimed that America had launched its revolution "as much for the benefit of the generality of mankind in Europe as for their own."[6]

Robert Kagan writes that revolutionary America did indeed win many contemporary admirers in Europe: "The American Revolution appeared as the first great political victory of the Enlightenment. Enlightenment *philosophes* in France, in Switzerland, in Belgium, in Germany, in the (Dutch) United Provinces, and in England saw in the American Revolution proof that their ideas were not merely theoretically attractive but could be put into practice."[7] If that were to come to pass, the American Declaration of Independence might also serve as a Declaration of Interdependence for a world order based on republican, cosmopolitan, and Enlightenment values.

———

However, applause in Europe came mostly from intellectuals who, in many cases, scorned their own governments. The political powers tended to look askance at these radical, provincial upstarts.

France was an exception. The French and the English had been at each other's throats for nearly five hundred years. Anything that worried Buckingham Palace raised spirits in the

Palace of Versailles. However, as bad luck would have it for the Americans, France and Britain were experiencing a rare if fragile calm. Not that King Louis XVI and his ministers were shedding any tears over the uprising across the Atlantic, but they were reluctant to plunge into another war with their historical enemy.

To coax France to the American side, the Continental Congress dispatched to Paris the American most renowned in the world, Benjamin Franklin. It might have been tempting for the founders to huddle at home in the years of war and the tumultuous decades of the fledgling government. But they were convinced that their survival required distant statesmanship of a caliber and standing that could be found only within their top ranks and deepest experience. Diplomats would have to make decisions on their own, since it took months to send orders from Philadelphia and dispatches from Europe. They would have to singlehandedly explain and convince Europeans that the American endeavor was just and in their interest.

———

The founders were all Atlanticists, and Franklin was the first of them all. His teenage sojourn to England had been exhilarating and formative, and his later missions, including two trips across the Channel, had made him all the more cosmopolitan. Even before the Revolution broke out, it was well known in Paris that Franklin had stood up to the British authorities during the row over taxation.[8]

Because his popularity among them had been paved during earlier missions, Parisian intellectuals swooned over *le rêve américain* well before the War of Independence. British North America had been a subject of fascination, admiration, and hope among French reformers.

Then there were the *philosophes* themselves, many of whom regarded Franklin as one of their own. Voltaire, in 1759, had echoed Locke's assertion of rights and anticipated the Declaration of Independence: "All men have an equal right to liberty, to the enjoyment of their own property, and to the protection of the laws."[9] Though he had never met Franklin, Voltaire heaped lavish praise on this intriguing character from the New World, comparing him to Newton and Galileo.[10]

Subsequently, Voltaire's frequent disputant, Jean-Jacques Rousseau, took both Locke and Voltaire to task for stopping short of replacing a monarchy with a republic, the only political system that he believed could live up to a legitimate social contract. Lacking that, "Man is born free and he is everywhere in chains."[11]

Many of the French saw America as a model for their own dreams of eradicating the connivance between the monarchy and the church. Denis Diderot, whose erudition was matched by pungent aphorisms, was credited with this zinger: "Men will never be free until the last king is strangled with the entrails of the last priest."[12]

Arriving in France at the age of seventy, Franklin wasted no time meeting with the foreign minister, Comte de Vergennes. They struck up a personal friendship, but from the outset they knew where the interests of their respective states met and where they diverged.

Three years earlier, Sir George Macartney, a statesman and colonial administrator, had exulted over "this vast empire on which the sun never sets and whose bounds nature has not yet ascertained."[13] Both France and America wanted to complicate Britain's imperial expansion, and France also thirsted for revenge for its defeat in the Seven Years' War.

Even though Vergennes served a king while Franklin was defying one, the foreign minister had already recommended to his sovereign in the spring of 1776, before the Declaration of Independence burst into the world, that France would be better off if the American Revolution prevailed.

Vergennes, ever so carefully, devised a plan to help General Washington with discreet loans and French officers seconded to the Continental Army. The most important was Gilbert du Motier de Lafayette. Even in his teens, he had single-minded determination to fight for the American cause.

It took Lafayette several months, with close shaves with the British, to make the journey. Washington would finally meet the nineteen-year-old Frenchman in August 1777, in his rank of major general in the Continental Army.

When Franklin arrived in Paris, he had one major goal—to achieve an alliance, nothing less. Vergennes acceded trade with America but stopped short of a military alliance.[14]

Undeterred, Franklin used a deft combination of patience and persistence, along with personality and reputation, to lay the groundwork for a breakthrough in French policy that America desperately needed. He established his own court in the pleasant, prosperous village of Passy, next to the Bois de Boulogne. His residence, a pavilion attached to a château with a magnificent garden, was America's first embassy.

Franklin's celebrity as a scientist made him irresistible. *L'ambassadeur electrique* dazzled his hosts with stories of his experimentations with kites, lightning rods, and batteries. They even forgave his poor attempts at French grammar and accent. His gregariousness, wit, and ingratiating manner masked his cunning, discipline, discretion, and relentless pursuit of his goals.

To keep the transatlantic dialogue going, Franklin arranged for public documents from home to be translated into French and widely disseminated. He wrote reports to colleagues back in Philadelphia and ghosted promotional material to make the American case to foreign audiences.

Some of these submissions were aimed at the Committee of Secret Correspondence. (Later renamed the Committee of Foreign Affairs, it would morph, in due course, into the State Department.) One such dispatch in April 1777 expressed his enthusiasm for expanding the scope of a permanent American diplomatic presence in other European nations: "We are glad to learn the Intention of Congress to send Ministers to the Empire, Prussia and Tuscany: With submission We think Holland,

Denmark, Sweden and Russia (if the Expence is no Objection) should not be neglected."[15]

To bolster that proposal, he launched into an early paean to the prospect of global leadership: "All Europe is for us. Our Articles of Confederation being by our means translated and published here have given an Appearance of Consistence and Firmness to the American States and Government, that begins to make them considerable."

When writing to friends back home, many of whom were suffering from the war, he sought to lift their spirits with assurance that America was on the right side of history. A letter to his friend Samuel Cooper, a Congregationalist minister, made that point: "'Tis a Common Observation here that our Cause is the Cause of all Mankind; and that we are fighting for their Liberty in defending our own."[16] In his autobiography, Franklin wrote, "We were fighting for the dignity and happiness of human nature. Glorious is it for the Americans to be call'd by Providence to this post of honour. Cursed and detested will everyone be that deserts or betrays it."[17]

One of Franklin's closest friends was Marie-Jean Caritat, Marquis de Condorcet, a philosopher and mathematician half his age. Condorcet was an ardent champion of "modern liberty," as distinct from ancient republics that granted the hoi polloi few civic rights. When the time came for eulogies for Franklin, Condorcet offered one of the most apt and succinct: "a man who believes in the power of reason and the reality of virtue."[18]

Throughout Franklin's first year in Paris, he continued to steward his relationship with Vergennes as the key intermediary to the royal court. According to one biographer, the foreign minister registered some irritation: "I really do not know what Franklin has come to do here," he remarked. When Franklin had first arrived, he had been occupied with a variety of projects. Since then, he seemed to "shut himself up in a sanctuary with the *philosophes*."[19] The quip was probably disingenuous, since he knew exactly what Franklin wanted, and it had nothing to do with ideology and philosophy. In conversation and correspondence with Vergennes, Franklin kept within the bounds of raison d'état. It almost went without saying that a France-America tandem would serve as counterweight to British naval power. He also alluded to the downside for France if America, lacking French help, had to accommodate British demands. He was careful, however, not to deliver an ultimatum lest the Americans appear desperate.

Franklin, the supreme realist, knew that his counterpart could not be gulled. Attempts to persuade Vergennes with speculative scenarios, whether rosy or disastrous, would be counterproductive. Success or failure at the negotiating table in Paris would depend on the odds of victory on battlefields an ocean away. While he understood the American endeavor, Vergennes could not oblige Franklin unless the tide of war turned against the British.

The reverse happened in September 1777. The British initiated a vast pincer movement that might jeopardize American victory. An immense force under General John Burgoyne crossed the Canadian border, making its way down the Lake Champlain region and the Hudson River valley. The plan was to hook up with General William Howe's army and fleet, severing New England from the south. But Howe had already occupied Philadelphia, compelling the Congress to move the seat of government to Lancaster and later York, Pennsylvania. That ominous blow had a personal sting for Franklin; a British captain commandeered and pilfered his house on Market Street.[20]

To counter anxiety in Paris with the arrival of this news, Franklin responded in the manner of a methodical, dispassionate scientist. He allowed for multiple contingencies. Yes, the enemy's massive, complex operation imperiled America; but it posed risks for Britain as well.

Franklin contemplated the permutations. Might the British underestimate the resistance waiting in upstate New York? Might Howe dally in Philadelphia rather than making haste north to reinforce Burgoyne? As it turned out, both came to pass. Howe had not followed his orders, camping out in Philadelphia and leaving Burgoyne marooned up north. Burgoyne, without Howe's forces to shore up his own, suffered a sound defeat in the Battle of Saratoga. Burgoyne surrendered on October 17, 1777, a year and ten days after Franklin had set sail for France.

The news reached Franklin on December 4, and he sent a message to Vergennes that same day:

Sir,

We have the Honour to acquaint your Excellency that we have just receiv'd an Express from Boston, in 30 Days, with Advice of the total Reduction of the Force under General Burgoyne, himself and his whole Army having surrendered themselves Prisoners. . . . Gen. Howe was in Possession of Philadelphia but having no Communication with his Fleet, it was hoped he would soon be reduced to submit to the same Terms with Burgoyne, whose Capitulation we enclose.[21]

Two days later, King Louis XVI invited the commissioners to open discussions on a formal alliance. After a year of playing hard to get, the French court was in a frenzy to negotiate a treaty.

Also in America's favor were the Saratoga rout's repercussions in Buckingham Palace and Westminster. King George III was both devastated and furious when he learned of the debacle. The mood in London was shifting toward the bleak conclusion that the war was not worth the huge financial costs and the military assets bogged down on the other side of the Atlantic.[22]

Even before a French-American alliance was consummated, Vergennes's earlier help with supplies to America's war effort forced Britain to contend with the enemy in the Caribbean. For the Americans, the operation was a sideshow, but her offshore loyal colonies were a major theater of defense for Britain.

Early in the conflict, Britain had offered palliative concessions, and many American colonists welcomed a compromise. Now London lowered the ante, although still on its own vague terms. The chief of the British secret service, Paul Wentworth, arranged a meeting with Franklin to sweeten the pot by granting America "unqualified independence."[23] However, Wentworth had a limited brief and could not elaborate on either the adjective or the noun. Franklin now had the high cards. He needled Wentworth: "Pity [the offer] did not come a little sooner."[24]

As the fortune was shifting, Franklin didn't mind that the word spread among gossips, journalists, and secret agents from various countries that the British were close to folding. If Britain sued for peace, it would put an end to a French-American alliance just when it would be to France's advantage.

Franklin wanted influential Parisiens not to be comfortable sitting on the fence, but he also put Vergennes at ease with an assurance of steadfast "reliance on the friendship of France," adding that the United States would "reject firmly all propositions [prejudicial to France] . . . with England which have not for their basis the entire freedom and independence of America."[25]

The king—who was also inclined to use the American victory against British power—directed Vergennes to negotiate the alliance, and France formally recognized the United States on February 6, 1778.

All of this was unknown to the delegates in the Continental Congress, who were gritting their teeth through another hard winter while Washington and his men struggled to stave off the bitter cold and the surrounding British at Valley Forge. Not until

April did the commander get the welcome word. The Washington biographer Ron Chernow recounts the moment: "At the news, Lafayette gave Washington—the man nobody touched—a double-barreled French kiss on both cheeks."[26]

Edmund Morgan, in *The Birth of the Republic*, marvels at Franklin's skill and patience: His was "the greatest diplomatic victory the United States has ever achieved" because it "won for Americans the foreign assistance which was the last element needed for victory."[27]

Benjamin Franklin had his own version of the art of the deal. For him, diplomacy required psychology and choreography, statesmanship and showmanship, waiting and acting, all in the context of reason and mastery of the facts.

———

The guns finally fell silent in North America when General Charles Cornwallis capitulated to American and French forces at Yorktown in October 1781. Legend has it that a British fife-and-drum corps was said to have played a seventeenth-century ballad with an undertone of protest against politicians back in London. The title of the ballad comes from the last five words in the refrain in all stanzas: "Yet let's be content, and the times lament, you see the world turn'd upside down."[28] The story, which may be apocryphal, persists in the lore of surrender ceremony.

Chernow believes that the Americans would not have prevailed in the Siege of Yorktown were it not for the Comte de Rochambeau, commander of the French expeditionary force.[29] In a supporting role and on instructions from Washington, Lafayette blocked the British army's escape from Yorktown by land while a French fleet cut them off by sea.

A hundred and thirty-six years later, a U.S. Army colonel, Charles Stanton, was part of the American expeditionary force that fought beside the French in World War I. In a speech, on July 4, 1917, he expressed America's gratitude for France's role in the War of Independence. He invoked a fellow officer, long-dead: "Lafayette, we are here!"[30]

———

George Washington, of course, was deeply appreciative of the French aid throughout the war. But in June 1783, when a formal peace with Britain was yet to be signed, he issued a circular letter to the states acknowledging the intellectual impetus to the American cause provided by bold thinkers in Europe—including, by obvious implication, Great Britain:

> The foundation of our Empire was not laid in the gloomy Age of ignorance and superstition, but at an Epocha when the rights of Mankind were better understood and more clearly defined, than at any former period—The researches of the human Mind after social happiness have been carried to a great extent, the treasures of knowledge acquired by the labours of Philosophers, Sages and Legislators, through a long succession of years, are laid open for our use and their collected wisdom may be happily applied in the establish-

ment of our forms of Government. The free cultivation of letters, the unbounded extension of Commerce, the progressive
Refinement of manners, the growing liberality of sentiment,
and, above all, the pure and benign light of Revelation, have
had a meliorating influence on Mankind and encreased the
blessings of Society.[31]

When King George heard that Washington was retiring to
his plantation, he was said to remark in astonishment, "If he does
that, he will be the greatest man in the world."[32]

———

By the time of Britain's final defeat, the mission and atmosphere
in Passy had changed dramatically, much to Benjamin Franklin's satisfaction. His hard work was mostly over, leaving him
more time to enjoy the overlapping social and intellectual life of
Paris. He kept abreast of the news of war and politics at home,
and, when necessary, tended to diplomatic business with the foreign ministry. But mainly he luxuriated in a movable feast, as
guest of honor, bon vivant, statesman, and, of course, *philosophe*.

Franklin had not met with Voltaire previously, but when he
returned as a diplomat, they came together publicly on two oc-
casions. The first was a ceremony in which Voltaire bestowed a
benediction on Franklin's younger grandson, Benny Bache. The
frail yet impish eighty-four-year-old savant—noted for his exco-
riation of Christianity—laid his hands on the boy's head and
intoned, in solemn English, "God and Liberty." A few months

later, just before Voltaire's death, the two met for the last time, embracing in the Académie Royale as adoring onlookers burst into acclamation.[33]

———

Since April 1778, John Adams had been part of the American delegation in Paris, but not by his own request. Nor did his fellow members in Congress give him the courtesy of accepting the assignment. Instead, they just notified him, assuming he would comply.

And they were right. After a short home leave in Braintree, Adams packed up, kissed the stoic Abigail, and, accompanied by their two sons—John Quincy, eleven, and Charles, nine—boarded the frigate *Boston*.

John Adams was already impressed by John Quincy's gifted intellect that might propel him into an exalted and beneficial career of his own. While in Philadelphia the year before, he wrote to the boy, urging him to read the history of the Peloponnesian War in the original Greek by Thucydides and Thomas Hobbes's English translation, which was in the Adams's family library:

> As the War in which your Country is engaged will probably hereafter attract your Attention, more than it does at this Time, and as the future Circumstances of your Country, may require other Wars, as well as Councils and Negotiations, similar to those which are now in Agitation, I wish

to turn your Thoughts early to such Studies, as will afford you the most solid Instruction and Improvement for the Part which may be allotted you to act on the Stage of Life.[34]

The winter crossing was harrowing. The ship survived frequent, violent storms and combat with a British merchantman. Soon after arriving in Paris, Adams became aware that he was in for another kind of misery. He was heralded by many Parisians who mistook him for his cousin Samuel, the storied hero of the Boston Tea Party, or the firebrand Tom Paine. When these mix-ups were clarified, he bewailed to his diary that he had become "a man of whom nobody had ever heard before,—a perfect cipher; a man who did not understand a word of French; awkward in his figure, awkward in his dress; no abilities."[35]

The more vexing problem was the twosome of Franklin and Vergennes. The cagey foreign minister had been won over by the celebrated personage from across the Atlantic. Vergennes, however, found the stiff-backed Adams rude and pushy—which he probably was, but for a good cause: persuading the French to deploy their formidable navy to hinder the British from wreaking havoc on the rebels up and down the Atlantic seaboard. When Adams refused to take no for an answer, Vergennes sent his ambassador in Philadelphia an order to persuade the Continental Congress to recall him. Franklin took Vergennes's side in a withering letter to Congress, stabbing his friend and fellow founder in the back.

Luckily for Adams, by the time Vergennes's and Franklin's poisonous letters reached Philadelphia, he had moved to Holland, a country he had long admired. So did others back home, who thought the Dutch were the most likely Europeans to support the American cause. After all, they had freed themselves from the Spanish throne and formed a republic in the early seventeenth century. They were well ahead of other European countries in the vexing and ubiquitous matter of religious freedom. The Dutch government took in the Puritans when they left their native land and separated from their king. They were welcomed in the university town of Leyden before moving to Massachusetts. Amsterdam had provided sanctuary for French and English freethinkers. Moreover, the United Provinces had also been quietly supplying weaponry to the emerging United States. Holland was a globalized nation of mariners and merchants with far-flung possessions and trade routes in the East and West Indies. Their settlements in the Hudson River valley had been absorbed into the British colonies.

Although the Dutch golden age was waning when the American War of Independence broke out, Holland's banks remained immensely wealthy and notoriously tightfisted. Adams had little success securing appointments with Amsterdam's lords of finance. He later referred to the city as "the capital of the reign of Mammon."[36]

The doors of the government in The Hague were also closed to him. This relatively unknown American without diplomatic rank was urging them to invest their treasure and risk the wrath of Britain to aid an army that was suffering a string of setbacks.

In fall of 1780, word had come of General Benedict Arnold's treason as well as British victories at Charleston and Camden in South Carolina. A Dutch confidant, admirer, and adviser, Baron Joan Derk Van der Capellen, told Adams that "never has the credit of America stood so low."[37]

Adams's mission was further hobbled when he came down with a mysterious, debilitating, and potentially lethal illness that laid him low for six weeks. His two young sons were unhappy in the strict, austere regimen at their school, and Charles, the younger one, also fell seriously ill. Upon his recovery, he suffered homesickness so severe that Adams decided to send him back to Abigail, which meant another harrowing voyage for the boy.

Although Congress, after much importuning by Adams, bestowed credentials designating him a minister plenipotentiary, the Dutch continued to stall. They were waiting to see whether the erstwhile American colonies would succeed in gaining their independence; and they were under constant warnings of retaliation from Britain if Holland aided the rebellion.

As though that were not enough, Adams's nemesis Vergennes was once again urging the Congress to recall him, this time from Holland, on the dubious grounds that Adams was complicating delicate European diplomacy. Vergennes and Franklin wanted France to be the sole European sponsor of America's independence.

When American and French troops defeated Cornwallis at Yorktown, Adams was elated. French naval assistance—which

he had been persistently advocating, to Vergennes's annoyance—
was a key factor in the victory. Even this turning point in the war
was not enough to open Amsterdam's banks' coffers for a loan,
and ministers in The Hague were still hemming and hawing
about whether to grant diplomatic recognition to the United
States.

Adams was fed up with knocking on Dutch doors only to be
sent away empty-handed. While he understood Holland's tick-
lish situation with its neighbors (as he put it, hopping about like a
frog between the legs of two battling bulls, France and Britain),
he suspected that there were powerful circles in The Hague par-
tial to Britain.

However, some influential Dutchmen leaned the other way.
His friend and counselor, Van der Capellen, issued a stern message to his countrymen: "I know the unflinching character of Mr.
Adams. I know that [Dutch rejection of his entreaties] has been
a sore point, and I shudder for the consequences if we embitter a
man of his influence, one of the principal founders of American
freedom."[38]

At this juncture, Adams rose to the occasion. With neither
permission nor support from Philadelphia, he took a bold step:
he went public with his case in a foreign land. As he confided
to his personal secretary, Francis Dana, America "has been too
long Silent in Europe. Her Cause is that of all Nations and all
Men: and it needs nothing but to be explained to be approved."[39]

Adams took delight in laying out the case for a Dutch-
American alliance, reminding his listeners and readers that the
two peoples were already bonded ideologically and geographi-

cally. He painted a rosy future of symbiotic commerce. His pamphlets and open letters about the emergence of a new country in the New World were disseminated around the Netherlands in English, French, and Dutch. On his travels from Leyden to The Hague, rather than spending his time at the ministries, he canvassed door-to-door the residents in the semiautonomous provinces. Adams's grassroots politicking worked in no small measure because of his decency, passion, and persistence. It was a masterstroke. Finally, the Seven United Provinces of the Netherlands vindicated Adams's fondness of this true republic. The Dutch people had voices of their own; they had ears to listen to this earnest, paunchy, silver-tongued foreigner; and they had eyes to read what he wrote to bring them to his country's side.

Late in February 1782, Friesland, a province in the north of the Netherlands, initiated a cascade of provincial votes in favor of Adams's status as minister of the United States. In April, Adams was received by His Most Serene Highness Prince of Orange, William V.[40]

While a consortium of Dutch banks released loans to the American government, the more important prize was Dutch recognition of the independence and legitimacy of the United States.[41] The Netherlands joined France in accepting this new nation, still at war with Britain, as among the powers of the earth. Adams wrote to Abigail, "If this had been the only Action of my Life, it would have been a Life well spent."[42]

With the wind at his back, Adams returned to Paris to join Franklin and John Jay, a New York lawyer and founder, to forge a treaty with Britain. Although the British were prepared to cease hostilities, they had balked at formally recognizing America's independence. But the Americans were persistent, deft, and ultimately successful.

———

With the war over, there might have been a consensus in Philadelphia to call back the founders from Europe to lend their prestige and wisdom in dealing with the opportunities and challenges on the home front.

Quite the contrary. Two familiar veterans from the previous congresses—Adams and Jefferson—were busy on the other side of the Atlantic. Adams, as minister to London, and Jefferson, as his counterpart to Paris, set a precedent, albeit unknowingly. Their three consecutive successors as chief executives would serve as diplomats overseas or secretaries of state or both: James Madison was Jefferson's secretary of state; James Monroe was minister to London and Madison's secretary of state; and John Quincy Adams was minister to the Netherlands, Prussia, and Russia and Monroe's secretary of state.

At no time since has a succession of presidents brought to that office such extensive and astute practice in foreign policy, both in war and peace. And at no time since has the nation been so vulnerable as it was in those early decades.

9

A Nation Born

The subject speaks its own importance; . . . nothing less than the existence of the Union, the safety and welfare of [its] parts . . . , the fate of an empire, in many respects, the most interesting in the world.

—*Alexander Hamilton*

The 1783 Treaty of Paris contained more than two thousand words, but for both parties, one sentence was the
most important: "His Britannic Majesty acknowledges the said
United States . . . to be free sovereign and independent states."[1]
That ultimate royal concession sufficed to satisfy Washington,
Jefferson, and Adams to declare an end to the war with Britain,
but it begged a critical question that only the victor could answer:
will the United States be a singular entity or a jigsaw puzzle of
sovereign mini-states? George III's advisers may have hoped for
the latter, but if the states were under the sway of an overriding
government, that would be another matter.

King George himself seemed resigned to a singularity—an
expanding country in another hemisphere that the world would
have to reckon with. On June 1, 1785, he received John Adams
for a private audience as the first American envoy to Britain. "I
will be very frank with you," His Majesty said. "I was the last
to consent to the Seperation: but the Seperation having been
made, and having become inevitable, I have always Said as I
say now, that I would be the first to meet the Friendship of the
United States as an independent Power."[2] Adams was stunned

and delighted, not least because he, too, envisioned his "country" as much more than Massachusetts.[3]

However, many Americans back home were wary of if not hostile to the thought of an overarching government for all the states. Southerners did not want northerners to have a voice in the future of slavery. Moreover, there was a wide suspicion, in both the North and the South, that a heavy-handed administration with a writ over all the states would curtail the rights that the states had just won.

That sentiment had been prevalent during the war itself. The Articles of Confederation and Perpetual Union, approved and ratified by Congress in 1781, guaranteed that each state would retain autonomy in a "league of friendship." The executive office of the confederation was subordinated to Congress and had a revolving door: ten occupants passed in and out during the eight-year phase (1781–1789). Having freed itself from an oppressive monarch three thousand miles away, America seemed to be opting for an enfeebled if not leaderless government.

———

James Madison, an up-and-coming Virginian in his thirties, along with two New Yorkers, John Jay and Alexander Hamilton, found this view to be shortsighted in the extreme without a real central authority. As America expanded geographically and demographically, the common affinities of the Revolution would weaken, and sectionalism would take hold.

Madison and his like-minded colleagues spearheaded a

campaign to replace the weak confederal system with a hybrid structure: the states would be partially self-governing but they would also be embedded in a nation with an administration able to assist and defend all Americans. The opposition was fierce. Officeholders in state capitals were more than satisfied with the status quo and mistrustful of ceding power to a national executive branch.

By fall of 1786, the advocates for a constitution were losing ground to the entrenched confederation forces. Madison and Jay resorted to the ultimate reinforcement by trying to enlist George Washington in their cause.

It was a long shot. The American Cincinnatus had been retired for three years and was determined to live an Arcadian life to the end of his days. In their correspondence with the squire of Mount Vernon, Jay and Madison were careful not to push him. Instead, they informed him that obdurate forces were jeopardizing the adoption of a robust constitution at a convention the following year.

Madison's language in a bill proposed to the Virginia House of Delegates conveyed rising alarm:

> [We] can no longer doubt that the crisis is arrived at which the good people of America are to decide the solemn question, whether they will by wise and magnanimous efforts reap the just fruits of that Independence . . . and of that Union which they have cemented with so much of their common blood; or whether by giving way to unmanly jealousies and prejudices, or to partial and transitory interests they will renounce the

auspicious blessings prepared for them by the Revolution, and furnish to its enemies an eventual triumph over those by whose virtue & valour it has been accomplished.[4]

During the war he also had been disgusted with the confusion and incompetence he had witnessed when dealing with the Confederation Congress. Three of his letters were particularly emphatic. To Hamilton, he wrote: "No man in the United States is, or can be more deeply impressed with the necessity of a reform in our present Confederation than myself."[5] To James Warren of Massachusetts, a guardian of the states' supremacy: "In a word, the Confederation appears to me to be little more than an empty sound, and Congress a nugatory body."[6] In another, to Madison, he went to the heart of the matter: "We are either a United people, or we are not. If the former, let us, in all matters of general concern act as a nation. . . . If we are not, let us no longer act a farce by pretending."[7]

In May 1787, George Washington did what Cincinnatus refused to do: he left his vine-and-fig-tree existence and went back to work for his country. He would be at it for another ten years.

———

Most of the delegates who came to Philadelphia thought they were there to revise the Articles of Confederation, but Madison and Hamilton were bent on a new document. They were determined to erect a sturdy structure that would bolster institutions and forge laws for a centralized government in balance with the reasonable perquisites and functions of the states. The founders of the United States deserved that entitlement because they laid the foundation—the ideological groundwork—for the republic. Their masterpiece was the Declaration of Independence, twelve years before. That document was a paean to unity, liberal values, and shared civic principles, providing the poetry for the American cause. The founders had provided the poetry. It was up to the framers to provide the prose.

The Federalists among the framers were up against the anti-Federalists, who stood for the primacy of the states and were trying to water down proposals for a robust nation. Tempers were frayed, voices raised, compromises pondered, and deals cut, only to fall apart in acrimony. A welcome if not saving factor for the framers throughout spring and early fall was Washington's magisterial presence as president of the convention. He intervened infrequently, but his votes yeah or nay on proposed articles signaled to the delegates that he was a committed Federalist.

In September, after four months of six-day weeks, the exhausted delegates prepared to take the final poll. The outcome was still hanging fire. A negative vote would have scuttled the document and risked the very existence of the republic. The framers turned to their patriarch, Benjamin Franklin. At the age of eighty-one and in constant pain from gout, he could not stand up from his chair, so a fellow member of the Pennsylvania delegation read the text to Washington and the delegates assembled in the hall. It was vintage Franklin, pragmatic and a bit playful. He warned that the perfect can be the enemy of the good; inflexible certitude can lead to autocracy; and opinion is not the same as truth:

> I confess that I do not entirely approve of this Constitution at present, but Sir, I am not sure I shall never approve it: For having lived long, I have experienced many Instances of being oblig'd, by better Information, or fuller Consideration, to change Opinions even on important Subjects, which I once thought right, but found to be otherwise. . . .
>
> In these sentiments, Sir, I agree to this Constitution with all its Faults, if they are such: because I think a General Government necessary for us, and there is no *Form* of Government but what may be a Blessing to the People if well administered; and I believe farther that this is likely to be well administered for a Course of Years, and can only end in Despotism. . . .
>
> It therefore astonishes me, Sir, to find this system approaching so near to Perfection as it does; and I think it will astonish our Enemies, who are waiting with Confidence to hear that our Councils are confounded, like those of the Builders of Babel, and that our States are on the Point of Separation, only to meet hereafter for the Purpose of cutting one another's Throats. Thus I consent, Sir, to this Constitution because I expect no better, and because I am not sure that it is not the best.[8]

Franklin's common sense, wry humor, self-deference, and skillful argumentation helped salvage the Constitution from failure. He was careful to mute his apprehension of what lay ahead should government fall into the hands of a despot. However, while slowly making his way out from the hall, he was buttonholed by a woman, probably Elizabeth Willing Powel, an influential figure in Philadelphia who presided over a salon for the political class. "Well, Doctor," she asked, "what have we got, a republic or a monarchy?" Franklin replied, "A republic, if you can keep it."[9]

Franklin's caveat was addressed to Americans who had decades to live as well as to future generations. He was warning *us*.

———

There was yet another hurdle to be crossed before the United States of America would become a constitutional republic. At least nine of the thirteen states had to ratify the Constitution. After the grinding, heated deliberations behind closed doors in Philadelphia, Madison and Hamilton joined Jay and went public with eighty-five essays under the rubric of *The Federalist*.

The concept of federalism arose from Cicero's vision of Rome not as an empire but as a cosmopolitan community based on a contract between the citizens and their leaders. The anti-Federalists believed that as a national jurisdiction grew larger, it would veer toward tyranny (for example, the British Crown), while republicanism could only thrive in self-sufficient entities (such as the Swiss cantons or Greek city-states).

Madison and Hamilton parried with their assurance that Federalist America would disperse appropriate executive, legislative, and judicial authorities to the states.

Once again, the European Enlightenment inspired the

American enterprise, especially by the *philosophes* Montesquieu and Rousseau and by David Hume.[10]

Hume, having in mind his native Scotland's uneasy relationship with England, made the most of what he believed was a universal human trait: "'Tis wisely ordain'd by Nature that private Connexions should commonly prevail over universal Views and Considerations; otherwise our Affections and Actions would be dissipated and lost. . . . Thus a small Benefit done to Ourselves, and our near Friends, excites more lively Sentiments of Love and Approbation than a great Benefit to a distant Common-wealth."[11]

Madison found that insight useful for understanding the states' responsibilities in a federal America. However, he insisted that the national government keep a vigilant eye out for trouble far from the capital: "The influence of factious leaders may kindle a flame within their particular States, but will be unable to spread a general conflagration through the other States. . . . [Any] improper or wicked project will be less apt to pervade the whole body of the Union than a particular member of it; in the same proportion as such a malady is more likely to taint a particular county or district, than an entire State."[12]

Madison was, of course, stipulating that powerful federal officials would be expected to extinguish, not fan, fires around the country.

———

Hamilton was less sanguine. In the first of the *Federalist Papers*, he warned that a dangerous ambition more often lurks behind the specious mask of zeal for the rights of the people, than under the forbidding appearance of zeal for the firmness and efficiency of government. History will teach us, that the former has been found a much more certain road to the introduction of despotism, than the latter, and that of those men who have overturned the liberties of republics the greatest number have begun their career, by paying an obsequious court to the people, commencing Demagogues and ending Tyrants.[13]

He returned to that concern several years later:

The truth unquestionably is, that the only path to a subversion of the republican system of the Country is, by flattering the prejudices of the people, and exciting their jealousies and apprehension, to throw affairs into confusion, and bring on the civil commotion. A man unprincipled in private life desperate in his fortune, bold in his temper, possessed of considerable talents, having the advantage of military habits—despotic in his ordinary demeanour—known to have scoffed in private at the principle of liberty.

Those then, who resist a confirmation of public order, are the true Artificers of monarchy—not that this is the intention of the generality of them. Yet it would not be difficult to lay the finger upon some of their party who may justly be suspected . . . when such a man is seen to mount the hobby horse of popularity—to join in the cry of danger to liberty—to take every opportunity of embarrassing the Gen-

eral Government & bringing it under suspicion—to flatter
and fall in with all the non sense of the zealots of the day—
It may justly be suspected that his object is to throw things
into confusion that he may "ride the storm and direct the
whirlwind."[14]

Of all the major founders' qualms about the future, Hamilton was most vivid—and most accurate—in his clairvoyance.

10

The Founding Creed

It is substantially true that virtue or morality is a
necessary spring of popular government.

—*George Washington in his farewell address*

The first American president was the savior of his country, a professional soldier, an aristocrat, and a slaveowner—a pedigree of a person who would ascend by acclamation to an office that might have come with a scepter and a throne. There were those who desired that outcome, while others feared the monarchical temptation. Instead, George Washington took seriously the title and role he had assumed at the Constitutional Convention: *presiding* over its deliberations. Now he was destined to preside over the deliberations of a country. He would guide, not rule. He would fulfill a duty but not pursue his own happiness, which he only found at Mount Vernon. Garry Wills has neatly nailed the paradox: Washington "gained power from his readiness to give it up."[1]

Yet he did something almost magical: he used his celebrity to make the American people believe that there was such a thing as an American nation, though the concept was, at best, a wispy hope for the future. Given his success in galvanizing a Continental army out of militias from thirteen colonies, banging on a beggar's bowl for the necessary funds, Washington already had a reputation for pulling together diverse entities, goals, and people who could imagine themselves as part of one cause and one land to that end. In his first year as president, he spent a month in New England, visiting sixty towns and hamlets.[2]

His rectitude was charismatic.

———

The political scientist James David Barber, in *The Presidential Character*, has written, "The Presidency is a peculiar office. The Founding Fathers left it extraordinarily loose in definition, partly because they trusted George Washington to invent a tradition as he went along."[3]

Washington was a proud man with a disciplined ego. While preparing for the presidency, he resisted grandiose titles that were suggested to him (Your Majesty, His Highness, the President of the United States and Protector of their Liberties). He refused a lifetime presidential post when one was proposed, and he was reluctant to serve a second term and contemplated resigning before the final four years were up.

Aware of his deficiencies and appreciative of others' skills, Washington was uncomfortable being treated as a demigod. Since the Constitution was mute on a cabinet, he established one of his own, consisting of five men. He recruited them based on his respect for their diverse opinions on what he called "interesting questions of National importance."[4] Rather than opening meetings with his own views, he listened to others before deciding on a course of action.

He was a virtuoso of silence. Often, he did not need to give an order. Instead, he let his subordinates deliberate among themselves, waiting for them to come up with a solution that he favored and then giving them the nod. He also convened meetings where he could solicit opinions and insights from men from different regions. Once he had surveyed others' opinions, he had confidence in his own judgment.

In his first inaugural address, Washington laid out his guiding principles:

> I behold the surest pledges, that as on one side, no local prejudices, or attachments; no seperate views, nor party animosities, will misdirect the comprehensive and equal eye which ought to watch over this great assemblage of communities and interests: so, on another, that the foundations of our National policy will be laid in the pure and immutable principles of private morality; and the pre-eminence of a free Government, be exemplified by all the attributes which can win the affections of its Citizens, and command the respect of the world.[5]

Washington believed that wise and benevolent statecraft relied on statesmen virtuous in their personal ethics: perspicacity, charity, and, above all, honesty with themselves as well as others. He wanted—indeed, insisted—that his closest colleagues hold to the same standard. Shortly after the inauguration, he wrote a note to Madison: "As the first of everything, *in our situation* will serve to establish a Precedent, it is devoutly wished on my part, that these precedents may be fixed on true principles."[6] The first precedents were cemented into the masterworks of the founders and framers.

A few days later, in a note to his vice president, John Adams, Washington set out guidelines for his successors: "The President in all matters of business & etiquette, can have no object but to demean himself in his public character, in such a manner as to maintain the dignity of Office. Washington added a particular trait that he frowned upon: *superciliousness*, a word that seems musty in the age of Twitter, but that suits America's tweeter in chief.[7]

———

Washington, the only president of the Revolution generation who had no formal education beyond elementary school, acquired a membership at the New York Society Library in his first year in office. The records show that he borrowed two hefty works in his first year: *The Law of Nations* by Emer de Vattel—a Swiss disciple of the seventeenth-century Dutch Enlightenment jurist Hugo Grotius—and a volume of recorded debates in the British House of Commons.[8] His selection of these tomes suggests what was on his mind: he wanted to learn about international governance in the Old World and the workings of the mother of all parliaments.

A newly inaugurated leader of a newly constituted republic was reverting to a habit from his long-ago youth: he was doing his homework.

———

Although he was stoic, Washington sometimes confessed to the loneliness, pressure, insecurity, and risks at the top. Early in his first term, he commented to Catharine Macaulay, an English Whig and historian sympathetic to the new republic, "I walk on untrodden ground. There is scarcely any action, whose motives may not be subject to a double interpretation. There is scarcely any part of my conduct [which] may not hereafter be drawn into precedent. Under such a view of the duties inherent to my arduous office, I could not but feel a diffidence in myself on the one hand; and an anxiety for the Community that every new arrangement should be made in the best possible manner on the other."[9]

There is an occasional touch of melancholy in his letters and the notes that his intimates took. Nevertheless, after eight years of coping with the vicissitudes that came with the office, Washington left to the five presidents who followed him an enduring model of leadership.

Washington's example was also imbued in the spirit and ethos of the times. All six lived in a period of unique opportunities and unique dangers. The Enlightenment was a common denominator of their schooling. In their band-of-brothers years, they took abstract ideas and fashioned them into something new, concrete, and applicable to the lives of people and the workings of a republic.

There is also the value of Washington's equation: personal

ethics and public ethics must be the same. Joseph Ellis, in his survey of the founders, puts it this way: "Honor mattered because character mattered. And character mattered because the fate of the American experiment with republican government still required virtuous leaders to survive. Eventually, the United States might develop into a nation of laws and established institutions capable of surviving corrupt or incompetent public officials. But it was not there yet."[10]

The visionaries of America managed to paper over their philosophical and personal differences for the sake of the greater goal of founding the republic.

But with the rise of political parties, which represented opposing ideologies, the cloak of comity began to wear thin. By 1792, Ron Chernow writes, "these selfless warriors of the Revolution and the sages of the Constitutional Convention had been forced to descend from their Olympian heights and adjust to a rougher world of everyday politics."[11]

Jefferson and Hamilton despised each other, and each wrote excoriating letters to Washington trying to get the other fired from the cabinet. Adams turned on Jefferson for his support of the French Revolution, with its bloody reign of terror. Jefferson, for his part, turned on Adams, beating him for a second term.

Adams snubbed Jefferson by slipping out of Washington in the early hours of his inauguration day, and there followed a sad silence of a dozen years between the two men. They had been partners during the writing of the Declaration of Independence and were close personal friends during the late 1780s, when Jefferson was minister to France and Adams was America's man in London.

The feud began to thaw on January 1, 1812, when Adams sent a cordial note to Jefferson at Monticello, beginning an exchange of 158 letters that lasted for fourteen years. Ellis, who has written biographies of both men, observes that they "knew they were sending letters to posterity as much as to each other."[12]

The scope of their correspondence seemed to probe almost every field of knowledge, much of it an extensive curriculum of the Enlightenment. On certain disputes of the past they found common ground; on others, they agreed to disagree. Disagreement, they knew, was not just inevitable: it was, and is, sacred ground for a democracy. A free people thrive on argument, as long as it has the spirit of dialogue.

"I have thus stated my opinion on a point on which we differ," Jefferson wrote, "not with a view to controversy, for we are both too old to change opinions which are the result of a long life of enquiry and reflection; but on the suggestion of a former letter of yours, that we ought not to die before we have explained ourselves to each other."[13]

A threatened friendship had been rescued, even though Jefferson and Adams never saw each other again. They stayed close to their homes, Monticello, Virginia, and Quincy, Massachusetts. Over the fourteen years of correspondence, their minds met regularly in a highly personal version of the Republic of Letters, and ended shortly before their deaths, within five hours of each other, on July 4th, 1826—the fiftieth anniversary of the Declaration of Independence.

Jefferson had directed that his gravestone note only his three proudest accomplishments: author of the Declaration of Independence, author of the Statute of Virginia for religious freedom, and father of the University of Virginia. Other contributions to his country and his world can be noted elsewhere.

As for Adams, he lived long enough to see his son John Quincy in the White House but was spared seeing him soundly beaten by Andrew Jackson. The Adams presidents, the second and sixth, were also the first and second to be voted out of office after one term.

———

With the passing of the Revolutionary generation, America entered a series of new eras. A few presidents rose to greatness, while others tried their best but failed. Even those who brought disgrace to the office paid lip service to the norms and laws that they skirted or violated. Why? Because they wanted to keep their niches in the pantheon that the founders had built for their successors.

Not Trump. He has used his tenure to construct a temple to himself. Now we know what happens when an extreme narcissist accrues extreme political power: he aspires for an earthly, personalized form of the divine right of kings. Freethinkers of the seventeenth century challenged that inane hubris. The American patriots rebelled against monarchy altogether. The framers did their best to forestall its revival.

The oath of office was a conspicuous ritual for that purpose. Before the inauguration address, the first words out of the president-elect's mouth were scripted by the framers and administered by the chief justice: "I do solemnly swear (or affirm) that I will faithfully execute the office of President of the United States, and will to the best of my ability, preserve, protect and defend the Constitution of the United States."

That's not a congratulation; it's a stern reminder of obedience to the framers.

The preamble of the Constitution starts with a capacious and unanimous plural pronoun: "We the People of the United States, in Order to form a more perfect Union, establish Justice, insure domestic Tranquility, provide for the common defen[s]e, promote the general Welfare, and secure the Blessings of Liberty to ourselves and our Posterity, do ordain and establish this Constitution for the United States of America."

A new president's own plans and goals must conform with the overarching ones of the framers. First and foremost was the aspiration of a cohesive nation. They knew that perfection is not in the reach of mortals. Hence, "a *more* perfect union."

An early and durable motto was *E pluribus unum*. It has often carried a dual meaning: the American states are united in a single country, and all citizens would have the same rights and responsibilities, regardless of ethnicity, gender, faith, and country of origin.

Trump has rejected both definitions. As candidate, he ran on a brazen platform of division and conflict. As president, he has used his powers to punish states likely to vote for his rival in November, and he has discriminated against Americans whose identity is other than that of his base.

The Declaration of Independence asserts only one identity: humanity.

Trump's version of "We the People" is "*my* people"—those who let him be their voice, while sneering at "*those* people."

As for justice, Trump dispenses rewards to those who please him and castigates those who don't.

And then there is another word, *Tranquility*, meaning civil peace. Trump has thrived on making enemies of his fellow citizens.

Thus, he has defiled *all* of the arch principles and virtues undergirding the supreme law of the land.

———

Trump has not only tried to adulterate American democracy to his solipsism—he has had considerable success. Four years ago, he cowed the Republican Party that had scorned him until its leaders surrendered to *his* leadership.

He has turned American foreign policy on its head and stuck it in the sand. He has cozied up to authoritarian regimes while diluting ties with allies who have shared America's traditional democratic values dating back to the founders themselves. How mournful it is to read the founders' determination, in the Declaration of Independence, to resist the "injuries and usurpations" of a tyrant and "[t]o prove this, let Facts be submitted to a candid world."

Today's candid world has resigned itself to dealing with a master of mendacity in the White House.

———

Not only is Trump the first modern president to scoff openly at the founders' ethics, ideology, and laws, he is the only one who has virtually jettisoned rational policymaking. He could get away with that as long as the issues at hand were in the realm of politics, laws, institutions, and the perversions of human agency. That's largely why Trump has such a dismal record of useful and senseful statecraft.

At the close of 2019, these bizarre stratagems had already achieved many of his desires, including a good chance for a second term.

Then a novel virus caught the entire globe by surprise.

Trump reacted as though he knew more than all of the medical experts. He had a campaign to run and win, and no one or nothing was going to stop him. He was used to staring down fellow beings, their laws, their institutions, their governments, but Mother Nature doesn't bend to bullying.

When nationwide protests against police brutality erupted in May 2020, again Trump was flailing. He lurched into a combative and bigoted mode, while Americans were overwhelmingly fighting for racial justice.

These two factors may have broken Trump's spell—but at a horrible price. And even if he is defeated, Trumpism will linger, and the wounds on the body politic will take time to heal. Still, having a normal president replace a grizzly bear would make it easier for Americans, in all our multiplicity, not to die before we have explained ourselves to one another.

Acknowledgments

Before I started writing this book, I read—and reread—
what the pros had to say about the Enlightenment and the
founding of America. I also contacted some of these authors,
who kindly responded to my questions.

Joseph J. Ellis has done far more than that. He has been
patient and generous in sharing his insights into the founders
and their times. His guidance over my shoulder has been indispensable. No wonder students and readers have revered him over
the decades.

I've known and admired Stephen G. Smith as a stalwart
friend and brilliant editor from our days at *Time* more than forty
years ago. As a history buff, he was instrumental in *Civilization*,
a magazine associated with the Library of Congress. He helped
me immensely with the prose and the narrative.

I'm also grateful for assistance from Rick Atkinson, David Blight, Eliot Cohen, Jill Lepore, Gary Saul Morson, Steven Nadler, Anthony Pagden, Javier Solana, Gordon Wood, and Antoine van Agtmael. Walter Isaacson and Patricia O'Toole reviewed the manuscript to its betterment.

Thanks to Bruce Carruthers and Ariel Gussie Schwartz of the Buffett Institute for Global Studies at Northwestern University. Their hospitality gave me an opportunity to meet impressive students and members of the faculty, including Garry Wills, who shared his perceptions of the European Enlightenment and the American Revolution.

I was offered a propitious fellowship at Institut Montaigne in Paris, thanks to Laurent Bigorgne and Alice Baudry. They arranged interviews for me with specialists: Antoine Lilti, a historian at the École des Hautes Études en Sciences Sociales, and Yves Citton, a professor of philosophy who has probed Spinoza's almost anonymous role in the American experiment.

My hosts also arranged a visit to Robert Badinter, France's former minister of justice who enacted the abolition of the death penalty. For years, he has been investigating many revealing facets of the French Revelation, including Thomas Jefferson's views and actions as minister in Paris during the upheaval. (When I walked from an apartment on the Left Bank to the Institut, I would tip my hat to the statue of Jefferson, where a pedestrian bridge crosses the Seine to the Tuileries Garden.)

Dominique Moïse, an eminent public intellectual, is also affiliated with the Institut. A friend of mine for many years, Dominique and his wife, Diana Pinto, are proof that the Enlightenment is still with us, despite the clouds on both sides of the Atlantic.

Nick Brown, principal of Linacre College at Oxford, gave me a chance to test the themes of this book in a Tanner Lecture. He also arranged for me to visit scholars at Christ Church, where John Locke was a student.

Jim Wertsch invited me to Washington University in St. Louis for a conference on "National Memory in a Time of Populism." He also brought me together with Abram Van Engen, a historian specializing in the British settlers of America in the seventeenth century.

Two teachers at Yale, Stephen Darwall and Steven B. Smith, explained the ancients' concepts that permeated the education and philosophy of the Enlightenment.

I'm also beholden to longtime friends who often gave me welcome guidance and encouragement: William Antholis, director of the Miller Center of Public Affairs at the University of Virginia, and Steven R. Weisman, a college classmate, journalist, author, mentor, and think-tanker.

Brookings has been my professional and intellectual home for eighteen years. I cannot imagine a more welcoming and edifying community. Many colleagues have helped me find my way forward. Their projects have influenced my own. Mike O'Hanlon gave me sound suggestions. I've learned much from Bill Galston in conversation and through his writings, especially a trenchant book on anti-pluralism, as well as from Susan Hennessey and Ben Wittes in their powerful dissection of what they call the unmaking of the presidency.

Phil Knight, a Brookings trustee and fellow scribbler, has been a friend for over a decade and has supported my work on this project.

The Brookings Library has been invaluable, thanks to Cy Behroozi, Laura Mooney, and Sara Chilton. I have also spent many hours in the Writers' Room on the fifth floor of the New York Society Library. The head librarian, Carolyn Waters, guided me through the stacks and records going back to the early Federal period when New York was the provisional capital of the nation. George Washington, John Adams, John Jay, and Alexander Hamilton availed themselves of the library's collection.

Ellen McCallister Clark—library director of the Society of the Cincinnati, a neighbor on Massachusetts Avenue in Washington—procured books and documents for my research.

Since I've been moving around, laptop-will-travel, I've been lucky to have the remote assistance of the magicians in Brookings's Information Technology, particularly Carlos Rondan and Amy Wong.

I'm grateful to Bill Finan, director of the Brookings Institution Press; Cecilia González, managing editor, who has overseen the production and tirelessly helped me with the manuscript and galleys; Katherine Kimball, a superb copyeditor; Elliott Beard, production manager; and Robert Wicks, publicity manager. Fred Dews of our Communications team partnered with me on this project as he has done over many years.

My greatest debt among the Brookings staff goes to Maggie Tennis. Over two years, she has been my indispensable collaborator, putting her considerable capacities to work in all phases of labor.

———

My sister Page, an inveterate Philadelphian, is a public historian who was chief curator of the Benjamin Franklin Tercentenary Exhibition. She shared her knowledge of the epic events in the Pennsylvania State House.

My brother-in-law, Mark Vershbow, has an uncommon gift for scrupulous logic and clarity. I have benefited from his honing of this manuscript. Rebecca Ascher-Walsh encouraged me from the first chapter to the last. Jordan Ascher, my step-grandson and a budding constitutional scholar, was an early reader who offered cogent advice.

My muse and greatest helpmate is my wife, Barbara Ascher. She is an accomplished author and natural editor. During the long slog for a short book, she kept me going in multiple ways, with a fine balance of reassurance and suggestions for improvements.

The founders often expressed their fears and hopes for posterity. So do many Americans today, frightened, for sure, but also hopeful. Barbara and I are in that category. We'll do what we can, but our children will probably have to expunge the pall so that their children can regain pride in our country.

Notes

Preface

1. The Woodward commission's report (*Responses of the Presidents to Charges of Misconduct*) was published by Delacorte Press in 1974.

2. Jill Lepore, "Measuring Presidents' Misdeeds," *The New Yorker,* September 3, 2018. Her resurrection of the Woodward book encouraged a new and expanded edition brought up to the Obama administration, and was edited by James M. Banner Jr., who was part of the original commission (*Presidential Misconduct: From George Washington to Today* [New York: New Press, 2019]).

Chapter 1

1. Charles Homans, "The 'Normalization' of Trump, and What Comes After," *New York Times Magazine*, November 1, 2016. Gingrich made this remark at a closed-door meeting of the Republican State Leadership Committee in February 2016.

2. Hillary Clinton, interview by Chuck Todd, *Meet the Press*, NBC, May 22, 2016.

3. Eliot A. Cohen, "The Age of Trump," *American Interest*, February 26, 2016.

4. Ibid.

5. Jonathan Freedland, "Welcome to the Age of Trump," *The Guardian*, May 16, 2016.

6. See Leslie Savan, "Words in the Age of Trump: Along with a New President, Americans Are Confronted with Coming to Grips with a New Vocabulary," *The Nation*, February 3, 2017.

7. Arthur M. Schlesinger Jr.'s three-volume biography of FDR, under the title *The Age of Roosevelt*, was published in the 1950s; Orville Vernon Burton's *The Age of Lincoln* in 2006; Sean Wilentz's *The Age of Reagan* in 2008; and William I. Hitchcock's *The Age of Eisenhower* in 2018.

8. As early as the 1970s, news outlets were stating that Trump graduated first in his class at the University of Pennsylvania's Wharton School. But reporters checked: Trump had never even made the dean's list. He has done nothing to dispel the rumor and has, in fact, encouraged it. Judy Klemesrud,"Donald Trump, Real Estate Promoter, Builds Image as He Buys Buildings," November 1, 1976; Dan Spinelli, "Why Penn Won't Talk about Donald Trump: As Trump Becomes University's Most Famous Alum, Campus Leaders Scramble to Protect the Brand," *Politico Magazine*, November 6, 2016; Justin Elliot, "Just What Kind of Student Was Donald Trump?," *Salon*, May 23, 2011.

9. See Jill Lepore, *The Whites of Their Eyes: The Tea Party's Revolution and the Battle over American History* (Princeton University Press, 2010). "For all the periwigs, the Tea Party's Revolution, in the wake of Barack Obama's election, had very little to do with anything that happened in the 1770s. . . . The Tea Party's Revolution was the product of a reactionary—and fanatical—version of American history that took hold during the crisis over the Bicentennial, a reaction to protests from the left," p. 68.

10. One example among many: James Hohmann, "Donald Trump Completes Hostile Takeover of Washington, Puts Both Parties on Notice," *Washington Post*, January 20, 2017.

11. Christi Parson, "In the Face of Trump's Attacks, Obama and

Other Ex-Presidents Remain Silent," *Los Angeles Times*, March 29, 2018. Although he avoided commenting on Trump's attacks, Obama campaigned vigorously for anti-Trump candidates in the midterm congressional and gubernatorial elections in 2018. Trump did extoll Ronald Reagan, who died in 2004, for talking tough during the 1980 election campaign on the Iranian confinement of the U.S. embassy staff in Tehran. He called Carter's handling of the situation a "disaster," one of Trump's favorite putdowns. "Remarks by President Trump in Press Conference, Osaka, Japan," June 29, 2019. But he excoriated Reagan when the latter was in office. See Michael D'Antonio, "When Donald Trump Hated Ronald Reagan," *Politico Magazine*, October 25, 2015.

12. Louisa Thomas, "America First, for Charles Lindbergh and Donald Trump," *New Yorker*, July 24, 2016. E-mail exchange with David Sanger, September 11, 2018.

13. Philip Bump, "Trump: 'Nobody's Ever Done a Better Job Than I'm Doing as President,'" *Washington Post*, September 4, 2018.

14. Kate Andersen Brower, "Former White House Residence Staff Appalled by Donald Trump's 'Real Dump' Comment," *Time*, August 2, 2017.

15. The press conference was held in New York during the United Nations General Assembly on September 26, 2018.

16. Trump's comments at rally, Lexington, Kentucky, November 4, 2019; broadcast that night on *Tucker Carlson Tonight*, Fox News.

17. See Jonathan Lemire, "Trump Makes Puzzling Claim about Andrew Jackson, Civil War," *Chicago Tribune*, May 1, 2017. Trump has demonstrated an anachronistic and garbled understanding of Andrew Jackson, slavery, and the Civil War. He has confounded scholars, who agree that slavery was the primary cause of the Civil War, by questioning the source of the North and South's conflict and wondering why it could not be "worked out." In his public remarks, Trump went off script on Jackson's "anger" over the Civil War, a puzzlement for those who knew that Jackson died sixteen years before the Confederacy opened fire on Fort Sumter. Interview with Donald Trump, *Washington Examiner*, May 1, 2017.

18. The designation *Enlightenment* came late, when most of the sages

who had personified it were dead. The Hanseatic philosopher Immanuel Kant coined the term (*Aufklärung* in German) in 1784, but it did not become commonplace in English until much later: the Encyclopedia Britannica first included an entry on the Enlightenment in its fourteenth edition, in 1929.

19. Henry Steele Commager, *The Empire of Reason: How Europe Imagined and America Realized the Enlightenment* (London: Orion, 2000), p. 101. See also Bernard Bailyn, *The Ideological Origins of the American Revolution*, fiftieth-anniversary ed. (The Belknap Press of Harvard University Press, 2017), pp. 26–27: "More directly influential [than Greco-Roman classics] in shaping the thought of the Revolutionary generation were the ideas and attitudes associated with the writings of the Enlightenment rationalism—writings that expressed not simply the rationalism of liberal reform but that of enlightenment conservatism as well"; Peter Gay, *The Enlightenment: An Interpretation*, vol. 1, *The Rise of Modern Paganism* (New York: Alfred A. Knopf, 1969), p. 2: "The substance of [the American founders'] ideas came from a handful of European thinkers"; James MacGregor Burns, *Fire and Light: How the Enlightenment Transformed Our World* (New York: St. Martin's Press, 2014), pp. xi–xii: "Although inevitably the Enlightenment took different forms from country to country and from generation to generation, in its dominant and pervasive ideas it transcended national and continental boundaries. Alike in the Old World and the New, it had its roots in the same intellectual soil, and produced a common harvest of ideas, attitudes and even programs."

20. This perspective—with its note of alarm—is the thesis of Robert Kagan's *The Jungle Grows Back* (New York: Alfred A. Knopf, 2019).

21. Joseph J. Ellis, *Passionate Sage: The Character and Legacy of John Adams* (New York: W. W. Norton, 1993), p. 241.

Chapter 2

Epigraph: *An Essay on Man*, 1733–1734.

1. Thomas Jefferson to Benjamin Rush, January 16, 1811, *The Papers of Thomas Jefferson, Retirement Series*, vol. 3, *August 12, 1810 to June*

17, 1811, edited by J. Jefferson Looney (Princeton: Princeton University Press, 2006), pp. 304–8.

2. "The free exercise of reason in matters of religious belief unrestrained by deference to authority; the adoption of the principles of a freethinker," *Oxford English Dictionary,* 2d ed., s.v. "free-thinking." First used in 1692, by S. Smith, in *The Religious Imposters.*

3. Thomas Paine, *Age of Reason: Being an Investigation of True and Fabulous Theology* (New York: Gramercy Books, 1993), p. 6.

4. John Adams, "A Dissertation on the Canon and the Feudal Law, no. 3," September 20, 1765, in *The Adams Papers, Papers of John Adams,* vol. 1, *September 1755–October 1773,* edited by Robert J. Taylor (Harvard University Press, 1977), pp. 118–23.

5. Scholars disagree over the precise death toll. R. J. Rummel, *Death by Government,* 5th ed. (Abingdon, U.K.: Routledge, 1997), p. 68, says between 2 million and 11 million. Norman Davies, *Europe: A History* (Oxford University Press, 1996), p. 568, puts it at 8 million. Steven Pinker, *The Better Angels of Our Nature* (New York: Viking Books, 2011), p. 142, suggests 5.75 million, more than double the death rate of World War I.

6. Anthony Pagden, *The Enlightenment: And Why it Still Matters* (Random House, 2013), p. 104.

7. Thomas Hobbes, in *Leviathan:* "Of the Vertues Commonly Called Intellectual," bk. 1, chap. 8; "Insignificant Speech," bk. 1, chap. 8, sec. 10; "Of Sense," bk. 1, chap. 1. In *De corpore* (On the body), Hobbes scorns "the gross errors of certain metaphysicians" who spout "meaningless vocal sounds, 'abstract substances,' 'separated essence,' and other similar ones." "Of the Passions of the Mind," in *Elements of Law, Natural and Politic,* edited by J. C. Gaskin (1640; Oxford University Press, 2008), bk. 2, chap. 9, sec. 13.

8. Quoted in A. P. Martinich, *Hobbes: A Biography* (Cambridge University Press, 2007), pp. 228, 355.

9. Hobbes, "Of the Passions of the Mind," in *The Elements of Law, Natural and Politic,* edited by J. C. Gaskin (1640; Oxford University Press, 2008), bk. 2, chap. 9, sec. 13.

10. Thomas Hobbes, *On the Citizen,* edited by Richard Tuck and Michael Silverthorne (Cambridge University Press, 1998), p. 3.

11. Donald Kagan, *The Peloponnesian War* (New York: Harper Perennial, 2005); Hal Brands and Charles Edel, *The Lessons of Tragedy: Statecraft and World Order* (Yale University Press, 2019).

12. Hobbes, *Leviathan*, introduction.

13. Hobbes, "Of the Rights of Soveraignes by Institution," in *Leviathan*, bk. 2, chap. 18.

14. In the *Leviathan* dedication, addressed to Francis Godolphin, a member of Parliament, Hobbes wrote: "I know not how the world will receive [the book], nor how it may reflect on those that shall seem to favor it. For in a way beset with those that contend, on one side for too great Liberty, and on the other side for too much Authority, 'tis hard to pass between the points of both unwounded."

15. Steven Nadler, *Spinoza: A Life* (Cambridge University Press, 2018), p. 160.

16. Baruch Spinoza, *Ethics*, pt. 5, prop. 19.

17. Jonathan Israel, *Radical Enlightenment: Philosophy and the Making of Modernity, 1650–1750* (Oxford University Press, 2001), p. 159.

18. Steven Nadler, *A Book Forged in Hell: Spinoza's Scandalous Treatise and the Birth of the Secular Age* (Princeton University Press, 2011), p. xv.

19. Catherine Drinker Bowen, *Miracle at Philadelphia* (New York: Little, Brown, 1986), p. 215.

20. Steven R. Weisman, *The Chosen Wars: How Judaism Became an American Religion* (New York: Simon and Schuster, 2018), p. 41.

21. Albrecht Fölsing, *Albert Einstein* (New York: Penguin, 1998), pp. 602, 728; Walter Isaacson, *Einstein: His World and Universe* (New York: Simon and Schuster, 2007), pp. 388–90. Einstein noted to Jewish acquaintances and the Catholic Church who criticized his spiritual beliefs that Spinoza had a similar but much harsher experience. The World Union of Deists (whose motto is God Gave Us Reason, Not Religion) has a page on its website devoted to Einstein quotations that supposedly affirm his deism. "Albert Einstein and Religion," www.deism.com/einstein.htm. However, none of them include the word *deism* or *deist*.

22. Baruch Spinoza, *Theologico-Political Treatise*, chap. 20.

23. Spinoza, *Theologico-Political Treatise*, chap. 20, para. 8.

24. Spinoza, *Theologico-Political Treatise*. chap. 20, para. 28.

25. Spinoza, *Theologico-Political Treatise*. chap. 20, para. 12. See also Steven B. Smith, *Spinoza's Book of Life; Freedom and Redemption in the "Ethics"* (Yale University Press, 2003).

26. Spinoza, *Political Treatise*, chap. 1, prop. 6.

27. Spinoza, *Theologico-Political Treatise*, chap. 18.

28. Spinoza, *Political Treatise*, chap. 7, prop. 27.

29. Spinoza's lungs were compromised from years of grinding optical lenses for a living and scientific experiments, and it is conjectured that he died from tuberculosis.

30. Baruch Spinoza, *Ethics*, pt. 4, prop. 67. Avishai Margalit (*New York Review of Books*, October 20, 2005) begins a review of Stuart Hampshire's *Spinoza and Spinozism* (Oxford University Press, 2005) as follows: "A friend visited the British philosopher Stuart Hampshire just before he died last year. Hampshire was able to talk only with difficulty but managed to say, 'Spinoza was right. In the end it is all biology.' The friend, as he was leaving, muttered politely, 'See you soon.' Hampshire replied, 'I don't think so.' He died the next day."

31. Karl Marx thought he had found in Spinoza's philosophy a version of historical materialism, and Nietzsche was intrigued with Spinoza from anthologies without reading any of his works. George Santayana, on the other hand, studied Spinoza's "master and model" seriously. His writings on Spinoza include an essay titled "Ultimate Religion."

32. Wim Klever, "Locke's Disguised Spinozism," Huenemanniac. https://huenemanniac.files.wordpress.com/2009/01/lockes-disguised-spinozism.pdf. Wim Klever, "Locke's Disguised Spinozism," *Revista Conatus: Filosofia de Spinoza*, vol. 5, no. 11, July 2010, pp. 41– 42.

33. Algernon Sidney, *Discourses concerning Government*, edited by Thomas West (Indianapolis: Liberty Classics, 1990): "God leaves to Man the choice of Forms in Government. . . . The general revolt of a Nation cannot be called a Rebellion. . . . Laws and constitutions ought to be weighed to constitute that which is most conducing to the establishment of justice and liberty," pp. 54, 392, 438.

34. *The Correspondence of John Locke*, vol. 2, edited by E. S. de Beer (Oxford, U.K.: Clarendon Press, 1975), p. 671. Referenced in Roger Woolhouse, *Locke: A Biography* (Cambridge University Press, 2007), p. 199.

35. John Locke, *Essay concerning Human Understanding*, in *The Works of John Locke in Nine Volumes*, 12th ed. (1689; London: Rivington, 1824), bk. 2, chap. 1, sec. 1.

36. Locke, *Essay concerning Human Understanding*, bk. 2, chap. 1, sec. 2.

37. Locke, *Essay concerning Human Understanding*, bk. 4, chap. 19, sec. 14.

38. Locke, *Essay concerning Human Understanding*, bk.1, chap.1, sec. 6. Locke writes of reason thus: "It is of great use to the sailor, to know the length of his line, though he cannot with it fathom all the depths of the ocean. It is well he knows that it is long enough to reach the bottom, at such places as are necessary to direct his voyage, and caution him against running upon shoals that may ruin him. Our business here is not to know all things, but those which concern our conduct. If we can find out those measures whereby a rational creature, put in that state in which man is in this world, may, and ought to govern his opinions, and actions depending thereon, we need not be troubled that some other things escape our knowledge."

39. Locke, *Essay concerning Human Understanding*, bk. 1, chap. 3, sec. 3. The Greek word *eudaimonia* (human flourishing) indicated the goal of an individual's life. Achieving that state required exhibiting virtue in thought and action—an exalted form of self-respect associated with the elite.

40. John Locke, *Two Treatises of Government*, in *The Works of John Locke*, bk. 2, chap. 2, sec. 4.

41. Locke, *Two Treatises of Government*, bk. 2, chap. 2, secs. 4–15, 54, 119–22, 163.

42. Locke, *Essay concerning Human Understanding*, bk. 4, chap. 18.

43. John Locke, *A Letter concerning Toleration*, in *Locke: Political Writings*, edited by David Wootton (Indianapolis: Hackett, 2003), p. 423. Referenced in James MacGregor Burns, *Fire and Light: How the Enlightenment Transformed Our World* (New York: St. Martin's Press, 2014), p. 37.

44. Locke, *Letter concerning Toleration*, p. 272.

45. Locke, *Letter concerning Toleration*, p. 390.

46. John Kenyon, *Revolution Principles: The Politics of Party, 1689–1720* (Cambridge University Press, 1977), p. 1.

47. John Locke, "The Epistle to the Reader," in *Essay concerning Human Understanding*, p. xiv.

48. Bernard Bailyn, *The Ideological Origins of the American Revolution*, fiftieth-anniversary ed. (Harvard University Press, 1992), v–vi.

Chapter 3

Epigraph: Alexis de Tocqueville, "Origin of the Anglo-Americans, and Its Importance in Relation to Their Future Condition," in *Democracy in America*, vol. 1, edited by John Canfield Spencer, translated by Henry Reeve (New York: G. Dearborn and Company, 1838), p. 9.

1. Virginia Bernhard, "Men, Women, and Children at Jamestown: Population and Gender in Early Virginia, 1607–1610," *Journal of Southern History* 58, no. 4 (November 1992), pp. 599–618; David R. Ransome, "Wives for Virginia, 1621," *William and Mary Quarterly* 48, no. 1 (January 1991), pp. 3–18.

2. Martha McCartney, "Virginia's First Africans," *Encyclopedia Virginia* (Charlottesville, Virginia Foundation for the Humanities, 2017). See also Engel Sluiter, "New Light on the '20. And Odd Negroes Arriving in Virginia, August 1619," *William and Mary Quarterly* 54, no. 2 (April 1997), pp. 395–98.

3. Charles Partree, *The Theology of John Calvin* (London: Westminster John Knox Press, 2008), pp. 240–52.

4. Samuel Danforth, a Puritan minister, poet, and astronomer, delivered a sermon titled "A Brief Recognition of New England's Errand into the Wilderness" in 1670. Perry Miller titled his history of the Puritans *Errand into the Wilderness* (The Belknap Press of Harvard University Press, 1964). Miller writes that American Puritans believed God "would bring back these temporary colonials to govern England," p. 11.

5. Edmund S. Morgan, *The Puritan Dilemma: The Story of John Winthrop*, 3rd ed. (New York: Library of American Biography, 2006), pp. 41–42.

6. There was a limited publication in 1838. The rediscovery came with Andrew Delbanco's *The Puritan Ordeal* (Harvard University Press, 1989), p. 72. A decade later, Peter Gomes, the chaplain at Harvard University, proclaimed Winthrop's message was not just "a definitive sermon" but a "formative moment" in the history of what would become the United States. Peter Gomes, "Best Sermon: A Pilgrim's Progress," *New York Times Magazine*, April 18, 1999.

Why, then, the deafening silence about it in contemporaneous chronicles, letters, and other documents that would have pinpointed on the map and the calendar precisely where and when Winthrop preached? Scholars have a speculative explanation: Winthrop's fellow voyagers who heard him preach were nodding their heads, moving their lips as he recited the biblical passages. But the sermon itself, eloquent though it was and of great interest to later generations, was nothing new to them. They were preoccupied with the mission and travails that lay ahead. See Abram Van Engen, "The Puritans Didn't Care about This Core U.S. Text," video, *Futurity.* See also Francis Bremer, "Christian Charity," in *John Winthrop: America's Forgotten Founding Father* (Oxford University Press, 2005), his "interlude" on the puzzling lack of accounts of the sermon.

7. For the text of the sermon in antiquated English, see John Winthrop, "A Modell of Christian Charity" (1630), in Collections of the Massachusetts Historical Society (Boston, 1838), 3rd series, vol. 7, pp. 31–48, Hanover Historical Texts Collection; for a redaction into modern English, see John Beardsley's version on the Winthrop Society website www.winthropsociety.com.

8. As Edmund Morgan puts it, the Puritan leaders "would effectively remove the colony from control by the Crown. The governmental powers of the company were extensive, greater in many ways than those which the King exercised in England. . . . Together they had established the first constitution for Massachusetts." Morgan, *Puritan Dilemma*, pp. 46, 83.

9. David D. Hall, *A Reforming People: Puritanism and the Transformation of the Public Life in New England* (New York: Alfred A. Knopf, 2011), p. xi.

10. John Winthrop, *Winthrop's Journal, "History of New England,"* *1630–1649*, vol. 1, edited by James Kendall Hosmer (New York: Charles Scribner's Sons, 1908), p. 75.

11. Francis Bremer, *John Winthrop: America's Forgotten Founding Father* (Oxford University Press, 2003), p. 355.

12. Stanley Lemons, "Roger Williams Champion of Religious Liberty," Providence City Archives, Providence, Rhode Island, archived from the original on May 29, 2014; Glenn W. LaFantasie, ed., *The Correspondence of Roger Williams*, vol. 2, *1654–1682* (Brown University Press, 1988), pp. 617–18.

13. Nathaniel B. Shurtleff, ed., *Records of the Governor and Company of the Massachusetts Bay in New England (1628–1686)*, vol. 1 (Boston: W. White, 1853, pp. 160–61.

14. James Davis Knowles, *Memoir of Roger Williams: The Founder of the State of Rhode-Island* (Boston: Lincoln and Edmands, 1834), pp. 74, 113.

15. Roger Williams to the Town of Providence, January 15, 1655, in *The Complete Writings of Roger Williams* (New York: Russell and Russell, 1963), vol. 6, pp. 278–79. See Jill Lepore, *These Truths: A History of the United States* (New York: W. W. Norton, 2018), p. 50. She traces Williams's metaphor of the ship to Plato's *Republic*.

16. John M. Barry, *Roger Williams and the Creation of the American Soul: Church, State, and the Birth of Liberty* (New York: Viking, 2012), p. 392.

17. Clifton E. Olmstead, *History of Religion in the United States* (Englewood Cliffs, N.J.: Prentice-Hall, 1960), pp. 5, 102–05.

18. Morgan, *Puritan Dilemma*, p. 120.

19. Timothy D. Hall and Mark C. Carnes, *Anne Hutchinson: Puritan Prophet* (Upper Saddle River, N.J.: Pearson, 2010), pp. 55–57.

20. Hall and Carnes, *Anne Hutchinson*, p. 77.

21. Winnifred King Rugg, *Unafraid: A Life of Anne Hutchinson* (Boston: Houghton Mifflin, 1930), pp. 109–11, 119. See also John Winthrop, *The Journal of John Winthrop, 1630–1649* (The Belknap Press of

Harvard University Press, 1996), p. 240; John Locke, *An Essay concerning Human Understanding*, in *The Works of John Locke in Nine Volumes*, 12th ed. (1689; London: Rivington, 1824), bk. 2, chap. 1, sec. 1.

22. Mark A. Graber and Howard Gillman, *The Complete American Constitutionalism*, vol. 1 (Oxford University Press, 2015), pp. 430–34.

23. Brandon Marie Miller, "Anne Hutchinson," in *Women of Colonial America: Thirteen Stories of Courage and Survival in the New World* (Chicago Review Press, 2016).

24. "John Winthrop: A Short Story of the Rise, Reigne, and Ruine of the Antinomians, Familists, and Libertines," in *The English Literatures of America, 1500-1800*, edited by Myra Jehlen and Michael Warner (New York: Routledge, 1997), p. 442.

25. Perry Miller, *The New England Mind: The Seventeenth Century*, vol. 1 (Harvard University Press, 1983), p. 391; Eva LaPlante, *American Jezebel: The Uncommon Life of Anne Hutchinson, the Woman Who Defied the Puritans* (HarperSanFrancisco, 2004), pp. 243–44.

26. Peter G. Gomes, "Anne Hutchinson: Brief Life of Harvard's 'Midwife': 1595–1643," *Harvard Magazine*, November/December 2002. See also Gary Boyd Roberts, *Ancestors of American Presidents* (Boston: C. Boyer, 3rd, 1989), p. 157; and Eva LaPlante, *The Uncommon Life of Anne Hutchinson*, edited by Gary Boyd Roberts (San Francisco: Harper-Collins, 2004), p. 243.

27. Thomas Hutchinson, *The History of the Colony of Massachuset's Bay: From the First Settlement Thereof in 1628, Until Its Incorporation . . . in 1691* (London: M. Richardson, 1765), p. 523.

28. Robert Winthrop, a senator from Massachusetts and distant ancestor of John Kerry, wrote a nineteenth-century biography of his forbear. Edmund Morgan ends his own biography with a tribute to Winthrop and a covenant elegy for the tightly knit community he left behind:

After his death, the colony did use its independence to become more and more provincial, more and more tribal, more and more isolationist; but the broader vision that Winthrop stood for could never be wholly subdued. No Puritan could be a Puritan and remain untouched by it, for it arose out of the central Puritan dilemma, the problem of doing right in a world that does wrong. Winthrop was not the last Puritan—or the last American—to wrestle with the problem or to reach an answer. There would be other men like him to open up the horizons when they became clouded by zeal or indifference. . . . On March 26 [1649] he reached what in life he had never sought, a separation from his sinful fellow men.

Puritan Dilemma, pp. 190–91.

29. "Copy of a Letter from King Charles the II to the Inhabitants of the Province of Maine, 1664," in *A Collection of Original Papers Relative to the History of the Colony of Massachusets-Bay, Boston, New-England: Printed by Thomas and John Fleet, 1769*, University of Oxford Text Archive. http://tei.it.ox.ac.uk/tcp/Texts-HTML/free/N08/N08849.html.

30. Michael Winship, *Hot Protestants: A History of Puritanism in England and America* (Yale University Press, 2019), pp. 290–92.

31. George Lincoln Burr, ed., *Narratives of the Witchcraft Cases, 1648–1706* (New York: C. Scribner's Sons, 1914), p. 218. More recent scholars resist the word *theocracy*, since the term denotes a society ruled by priests and ministers, and the Puritan leaders presiding over legislative and civic duties could not be drawn from the class of ordained ministers. Church leaders and civic leaders worked closely with one another, but were seen as having separate roles.

32. Joseph J. Ellis, *American Dialogue: The Founders and Us* (New York: Alfred A. Knopf, 2018), pp. 223–25.

33. Thomas Hobbes, "Of the Naturall Condition of Mankind," in *Leviathan*, bk. 1, chap. 13.

34. Locke, *Two Treatises of Government*, Chap. V, §§ 49.

35. William Christie Macleod, *The American Indian Frontier* (London: Dawsons of Pall Mall, 1968), pp. 175–78; David Treuer, *The Heartbeat of Wounded Knee: Native America from 1890 to the Present* (New York: Riverhead Books, 2019), pp. 39–51.

36. See Caroline Winterer, *American Enlightenments: Pursuing Happiness in the Age of Reason* (Yale University Press, 2016), p. 13. She

calls Locke's sentence "a text whose vision of the first, primordial human societies was dependent on [his] secondhand knowledge of the American setting."

37. See Mary Nyquist, "Hobbes, Slavery, and Despotical Rule," *Representations* 106, no. 1 (Spring 2009), pp. 1–33. In her abstract (p. 1), she writes,

> Hobbes's theorization of contractual absolutism relies upon a juridico-military doctrine relating to the enslavement of war captives, a doctrine that for Grotius has the authority of the law of nations. Although Hobbes's appeal to this doctrine cannot be understood apart from contemporaneous rhetorical appeals to figurative 'slavery,' his representation of a dramatic encounter involving the military victor's power of life and death enables him to develop novel views of civil subjecthood and of the family, together with a defense of Atlantic slavery that is later appropriated by Locke.

38. In the Second Treatise of Government, Locke seems to have denounced slavery in one passage ("natural liberty of man is to be free from any superior power on earth," *Two Treatises of Government*, bk. 2, chap. 4, sec. 22), but elsewhere he contorts and contradicts himself with two shaky exceptions. The first case is his suggestion that slavery might be a humane alternative to capital punishment. In the second, he echoes Hobbes, suggesting it would be acceptable to enslave prisoners abducted in a "just war," meaning a war started by the captives themselves.

39. *Fundamental Constitutions of Carolina*, March 1, 1669, Avalon Project at Yale Law School. http://avalon.law.yale.edu/17th_century/nc05 .asp. See also David Armitage, "John Locke, Carolina, and the *Two Treatises of Government*," *Political Theory* 32, no. 5 (October 2004), pp. 602–27.

40. Isaac Newton was also involved in the slave trade. He invested in the London-based South Sea Company while it was the hottest stock around and made a fortune, only to see it evaporate when the company collapsed in the market crash known as the South Sea bubble. Hobbes held stock in the early 1720s in the Virginia Company and the Somers Island Company.

41. Charles W. Mills, *The Racial Contract* (Cornell University Press, 2014), p. 68; Mary Nyquist, "Hobbes, Slavery, and Despotical Rule," *Representations*, vol. 107, no. 1 (Spring, 2009), p. 22; Urmila Sharma and S. K. Sharma, *Western Political Thought* (Washington, D.C.: Atlantic Publishers, 2006), p. 440; Deborah Baumgold, "Slavery Discourse before the Restoration: The Barbary Coast, Justinian's Digest, and Hobbes's Political Theory," *History of European Ideas*, vol. 36, no. 4 (2010), p. 412.

Chapter 4

Epigraph: Josiah Quincy, *Memoir of the Life of Josiah Quincy, Junior, of Massachusetts Bay, 1744–1775*, third edition, edited by Eliza Susan Quincy (Boston: Little, Brown, and Company, 1875), p. 289.

1. Walter Isaacson, introduction to *Benjamin Franklin: In Search of a Better World* (Yale University Press, 2005), p. 2.

2. Walter Isaacson, *Benjamin Franklin: An American Life* (New York: Simon and Schuster, 2003), p. 17.

3. James Gilreath, "American Book Distribution," *Proceedings of the American Antiquarian Society*, vol. 95 (October 1985), pp. 501–83.

4. Jill Lepore, *The Book of Ages: The Life and Opinions of Jane Franklin* (New York: Alfred A. Knopf/Penguin Random House), p. 20, referencing L. A. Lemay, *The Life of Benjamin Franklin*, vol. 1 (University of Pennsylvania Press, 2006), p. 57.

5. According to Kenneth Lockridge's *Literacy in Colonial New England: An Enquiry into the Social Context of Literacy in the Early Modern West* (New York: W. W. Norton, 1979), 90 percent of males in New England were literate, while the rate among women was 50 percent. Both numbers were lower in the South.

6. Isaacson, *Benjamin Franklin*, pp. 8–9. See also Nick Bunker, *Young Benjamin Franklin: The Birth of Ingenuity* (New York: Alfred A. Knopf, 2018), pp. 46–47.

7. Benjamin Franklin, *The Autobiography of Benjamin Franklin* (New York: P. F. Collier, 1909), p. 13–14.

8. Isaacson, *Benjamin Franklin*, p. 25.

9. Ralph L. Ketcham, *Benjamin Franklin* (New York: Twayne Publishers, 1965), pp. 9, 17–22.

10. Franklin, *Autobiography*, p. 14.

11. Daniel Defoe, introduction to *An Essay upon Projects*, edited by Henry Morley (London: Cassell, 1887).

12. Tomás Maldonado, "Defoe and the 'Projecting Age,'" *Design issues* 18, no. 1 (Winter 2002), pp. 78–85.

13. Library Company of Philadelphia, *Annual Report for the Year 1969* (Philadelphia, The Library Company of Philadelphia, 1970), p. 23. Also see *Poor Richard's Books: An Exhibition of Books owned by Benjamin Franklin Now on the Shelves of the Library Company of Philadelphia*, compiled by James Green (Philadelphia: Library Company of Philadelphia, 1990), p. 39.

14. Thomas S. Kidd, *Benjamin Franklin: The Religious Life of a Founding Father* (Yale University Press, 2017), p. 26.

15. "No. 10," *The Spectator*, March 12, 1711.

16. Franklin, *Autobiography*, p. 20. Also see Isaacson, *Benjamin Franklin*, p. 34.

17. Isaacson, *Benjamin Franklin*, p. 34; Bunker, *Young Benjamin Franklin*, pp. 121–23, 153–54; Lepore, *Book of Ages*, p. 38.

18. J. A. Leo Lemay, *The Life of Benjamin Franklin*, vol. 1 (University of Pennsylvania Press, 2006), p. 120; cited in Lepore, *Book of Ages*, p. 35.

19. For James's retort, see issue 18 of the *New-England Courant*, December 4, 1721; cited in Lepore, *Book of Ages*, p. 35.

20. "Ann Smith Franklin," Princeton University Library, February 16, 2004. (http://libweb2.princeton.edu/rbsc2/ga/unseenhands/printers/Franklin.html).

21. Franklin, *Autobiography*, p. 55:

My Parents had early given me religious Impressions, and brought me through my Childhood piously in the Dissenting Way. But I was scarce 15 when, after doubting by turns of several Points as I found them disputed in the different Books I read, I began to doubt of Revelation itself. Some Books against Deism fell into my Hands; they were said to be the Substance of Sermons preached at Boyle's Lectures. It happened that they wrought an Effect on me quite contrary to what was intended by them: For the Arguments of the Deists which were quoted to be refuted, appeared to me much Stronger than the Refutations. In short I soon became a thorough Deist.

22. Bunker, *Young Benjamin Franklin*, pp. 96–97, and Roger Woolhouse, *Locke: A Biography* (Cambridge University Press, 2007), pp. 436–38.

23. Antoine Arnauld and Pierre Nicole, *Logic, or, the Art of Thinking*, translated into English by John Ozell (Cambridge University Press, 1996). A copy with Franklin's signature on the title page is in the Library Company of Philadelphia's collection.

24. Franklin, as a writer, was a gifted ventriloquist, as his columns for the *New-England Courant* under the pen name Mrs. Silence Dogood attest. Mrs. Dogood was unschooled but highly literate ("I took a more than ordinary Delight in reading ingenious Books") with no reverence for pious dogma ("A Man compounded of Law and Gospel, is able to cheat a whole Country with his Religion . . ."). "Silence Dogood #1," *New-England Courant*, April 2, 1722; "Silence Dogood #9," *New-England Courant*, July 23, 1722.

25. Benjamin Franklin, *A Dissertation on Liberty and Necessity* (1725), in *The Papers of Benjamin Franklin*, vol. 1, *January 6, 1706 through December 31, 1734*, edited by Leonard W. Labaree (Yale University Press, 1959).

26. Franklin, *Autobiography*, pp. 42.

27. Nick Bunker, *Young Benjamin Franklin: The Birth of Ingenuity* (New York: Alfred A. Knopf, 2018), pp. 176–77.

28. In 1730 Franklin published an anonymous letter in the *Pennsylvania Gazette* satirizing those who castigated "blasphemous" philosophers:

Sir: I know well that the Age in which we live, abounds in Spinosists, *Hobbists*, and *most impious Free-Thinkers*, who despise *Revelation*, and treat the *most sacred Truths* with Ridicule and *Contempt*:

Nay, to such an Height of Iniquity are they arrived, that they not only deny the *Existence* of the *Devil*, and of *Spirits* in general. . . . [But] I do, indeed, confess that the Arguments of some of these unbelieving Gentlemen, with whom I have heretofore conversed on the Subject of *Spirits*, Apparitions, *Witches*, &c. carried with them a great Sh[o]w of Reason, and were so specious, that I was strongly inclined to think them in the Right; and for several Years past have lived without any Fear or Apprehensions of *Daemons* or *Hobgoblins*.

"Letter of the Drum," *Pennsylvania Gazette*, April 23,1730. See Kidd, *Benjamin Franklin: The Religious Life*, pp. 86–87, 201; and Leo Lemay, ed., *Franklin: Writings* (Literary Classics of the United States, 1987), p. 145; for Franklin's authorship of the letter, see Leo Lemay, *The Canon of Benjamin Franklin, 1722–1776: New Attributions and Reconsiderations* (Newark: University of Delaware Press,1986), pp. 42–43.

29. Franklin, "On the Providence of God in the Government of the World, 1732," *The Papers of Benjamin Franklin*, vol. 1, *January 6, 1706 through December 31, 1734*, edited by Leonard W. Labaree (New Haven: Yale University Press, 1959), pp. 264–69.

30. Benjamin Franklin to John Franklin, 1–31 May 1745, *The Papers of Benjamin Franklin*, vol. 3, *January 1, 1745, through June 30, 1750*, edited by Leonard W. Labaree (Yale University Press, 1961), pp. 26–27; Isaacson, *Benjamin Franklin*, pp. 86–87.

31. Benjamin Franklin to Benjamin Vaughan, 9 November 1779, *The Papers of Benjamin Franklin*, vol. 31, *November 1, 1779, through February 29, 1780*, edited by Barbara B. Oberg (Yale University Press, 1995), pp. 57–60.

32. Isaacson, *Benjamin Franklin*, p. 83. Howard Markel, a physician and professor of the history of medicine at the University of Michigan, wrote an op-ed for the *New York Times*, titled "Life, Liberty, and the Pursuit of Vaccines," February 28, 2011, noting that Philadelphia was already a mecca of new discoveries and practices in medicine. A rueful passage in Franklin's autobiography explains his cause against the disease: "In 1736 I lost one of my sons, a fine boy of four years old, by the small-pox, taken

in the common way. I long regretted bitterly, and still regret that I had not given it to him by inoculation. This I mention for the sake of parents who omit that operation, on the supposition that they should never forgive themselves if a child died under it; my example showing that the regret may be the same either way, and that, therefore, the safer should be chosen." Franklin, *Autobiography*, 96.

33. Isaacson, *Benjamin Franklin*, p. 150. In 1851 the population of the United States surpassed that of the United Kingdom.

34. Benjamin Franklin, "Apology for Printers," *Pennsylvania Gazette*, June 1731.

35. The Loganian Library, founded August 28, 1754. https://founders.archives.gov/documents/Franklin/01-05-02-0113.

36. Benjamin Franklin, "A Proposal for Promoting Useful Knowledge," 14 May 1743, in *The Papers of Benjamin Franklin*, vol. 2, *January 1, 1735, through December 31, 1744*, edited by Leonard W. Labaree (Yale University Press, 1961), pp. 378–83.

37. Harvard College, established in 1636 by Puritans to train clergy for the Massachusetts Bay Colony, was the first. In 1693 the colonial government of Virginia petitioned King William and Queen Mary—the coregents who made it possible for John Locke to return from Holland—to charter a college in their name. The College of William and Mary was followed in 1701 by a "collegiate school" for Congregational clergy in Connecticut that was named after a benefactor on the other side of the globe, Elihu Yale, the British governor of the East India Company in Madras (another prominent Britain who reaped some of his fortune from the slave trade). Rhode Island College (now Brown University, whose founding family and early governing board were also tied to slavery and the slave trade), King's College (now Columbia University, established in 1754), St. John's College (formerly King William's School, established in 1696), Moravian College, the University of Delaware (formerly Newark College, established 1832), the College of New Jersey (now Princeton University, established 1746), and Hampden-Sydney College in 1775, named, in part, after the English reformer Algernon Sidney, who was executed for his antimonarchal views. (The founders of the college used the alternative spelling of the name.)

38. Isaacson, *Benjamin Franklin*, pp. 146–47, 438.

39. Harvard and Yale gave Franklin honorary master's degrees, and near the end of his life, Franklin College was founded in Lancaster, Pennsylvania (the name of John Marshall, the fourth chief justice of the United States, was added later).

Chapter 5

Epigraph: King George III quoted in Rick Atkinson, *The British Are Coming: The War for America, Lexington to Princeton* (New York: Henry Holt, 2019).

1. Joseph Ellis, *His Excellency: George Washington* (New York: Alfred A. Knopf, 2004), p. 7.

2. H. W. Brands, *The First American: The Life and Times of Benjamin Franklin* (New York: Anchor Books, 2000), pp. 263–71.

3. George Washington to John Augustine Washington, 31 May 1754, *The Papers of George Washington*, Colonial Series, vol. 1, *7 July 1748–14 August 1755*, edited by W. W. Abbot (University Press of Virginia, 1983), pp. 118–19; Kevin J. Hayes, *George Washington: A Life in Books* (Oxford University Press, 2017), p. 79.

4. Ellis, *His Excellency*, pp. 13–14.

5. Peter R. Henriques, *Realistic Visionary: A Portrait of George Washington* (Charlottesville and London: University of Virginia Press, 2006), p. 6.

6. Walter Isaacson, *Benjamin Franklin: An American Life* (Yale University Press, 2005), p. 166.

7. Benjamin Franklin, *The Autobiography of Benjamin Franklin* (New York: P. F. Collier, 1909), p. 136.

8. Ron Chernow, *Washington: A Life* (New York: Penguin, 2010), p. 65; Kevin J. Hayes, *George Washington: A Life in Books* (Oxford University Press, 2017), p. 177.

9. The theaters were Europe, the Americas, West Africa, the Indian subcontinent, and Southeast Asia (the Philippines). Britain, Portugal, Prussia, and smaller German states squared off against France, Spain, Sweden, and the Holy Roman, Russian, and Mughal Empires.

10. Robert Kagan, *Dangerous Nation: America's Place in the World from Its Earliest Days to the Dawn of the Twentieth Century* (New York: Alfred A. Knopf, 2006), p. 26: "The spark that ignited the destructive Seven Years' War, however, came not from any action in London but from the colonies." Also see Fred Anderson, *Crucible of War: The Seven Years' War and the Fate of Empire in British North America, 1754–1766* (New York: Knopf Doubleday, 2007), p. 1: "That the greatest of Europe's eighteenth-century wars could have begun in the Pennsylvania backcountry reflected the growing importance of America in the diplomatic, military, and economic calculations of European governments. That it spread as it did from the New World to the Old resulted from the maneuverings of European diplomats who, seeking advantage, destroyed the fragile balance of power established by the Treaty of Aix-la-Chapelle (1748) at the end of the previous war." France ceded the Louisiana Territory to Spain. In 1801, the land was transferred back to France as part of a secret treaty signed between the French and Spanish.

11. Peter D. G. Thomas, "The Cost of the British Army in North America, 1763–1775," *William and Mary Quarterly* 45, no. 3 (1988), pp. 510–16.

12. "Examination before the Committee of the Whole of the House of Commons, 13 February 1766," in *The Papers of Benjamin Franklin*, vol. 13, *January 1 through December 31, 1766*, edited by Leonard W. Labaree (Yale University Press, 1969), pp. 124–62; Isaacson, *Benjamin Franklin*, p. 230.

13. John Adams to Nathan Webb, with Comments by the Writer Recorded in 1807, *The Adams Papers, Papers of John Adams*, vol. 1, *September 1755–October 1773*, edited by Robert J. Taylor (Harvard University Press, 1977), pp. 4–7.

14. Adams to Webb, with Comments by the Writer. The "exactest computations" was Adams's reference to Franklin's "Observations Concerning the Increase of Mankind."

15. John Adams, "A Dissertation on the Canon and the Feudal Law," No. 4, 21 October 1765, *The Adams Papers, Papers of John Adams*, vol. 1, *September 1755–October 1773*, edited by Robert J. Taylor (Harvard University Press, 1977), pp. 123–28.

16. Adams, "A Dissertation on the Canon and the Feudal Law," No. 4, 21 October 1765.

17. Diary of John Adams, Diary 11, entry for December 18, 1765, Adams Family Papers, Massachusetts Historical Society. Also see David McCullough, *John Adams* (New York: Simon and Schuster, 2001), p. 62.

18. Adams, "A Dissertation on the Canon and the Feudal Law," No. 4, 21 October 1765.

19. John Adams, *Discourses on Davila*, in *The Works of John Adams, Second President of the United States*, edited by Charles Francis Adams, vol. 6, *Defence of the Constitutions Vol. III cont'd, Davila, Essays on the Constitution* (Boston: Little, Brown, 1856), pp. 243–44.

20. Benjamin Franklin to Robert R. Livingston, 22 July 1783, *The Adams Papers, Adams Family Correspondence*, vol. 5, *October 1782–November 1784*, edited by Richard Alan Ryerson (Harvard University Press, 1993), pp. 251–52.

21. Adams, *Discourses on Davila*, p. 279.

22. Francis Hutcheson, *A Short Introduction to Moral Philosophy*, in *Three Books*, bk. 3, chap. 6 (Glasgow, 1747), p. 298.

23. Joseph J. Ellis, *American Sphinx: The Character of Thomas Jefferson* (New York: Alfred A. Knopf, 1998), p. 67.

24. Thomas Jefferson to Louis H. Girardin, 15 January 1815, *The Papers of Thomas Jefferson: Retirement Series*, vol. 8, *1 October 1814 to 31 August 1815*, edited by J. Jefferson Looney (Princeton University Press, 2011), pp. 200–201.

25. Thomas Jefferson, *Autobiography*, in *The Writings of Thomas Jefferson*, vol. 1, edited by H. A. Washington (Cambridge University Press, 2011), p. 2.

26. That was the term for the French philosophers of the eighteenth century, who prided themselves on their individualistic and argumentative brilliance.

27. Jon Meacham, *Thomas Jefferson: The Art of Power* (New York: Random House, 2012); Gillian Hull, "William Small 1734–1775: No Publications, Much Influence," *Journal of the Royal Society of Medicine*, 90, no. 2 (1997): 102–05.

28. William Wirt Henry, *Life, Correspondence, and Speeches*, vol. 1 (New York: Charles Scribner's Sons, 1891), p. 86; Meacham, *Jefferson*, p. 32.

29. It was common for someone of Jefferson's generation to use the word *country* in that context, and he carried the habit to his grave. His autobiography, written when he was seventy-seven, often used "country" for Virginia as well as for the United States.

30. Meacham, *Jefferson*, pp. 38–39.

31. Patrick Henry, quoted in John Adams Diary 22A, "Notes of Debates in the Continental Congress, 6 September 1774," Adams Family Papers, Massachusetts Historical Society.

32. Parliament of Great Britain, An Act Repealing the Stamp Act (March 18, 1766), Yale Law School, Lillian Goldman Law Library (2008), Avalon Project.

33. Brands, *The First American*, pp. 4–7.

Chapter 6

Epigraph: John Adams, *The Works of John Adams: Second President of the United States*, edited by Charles Francis Adams, vol. 2, *Diary, Notes of Debates, Autobiography* (Boston: Little, Brown, 1850), diary entry for November 9, 1774, p. 405.

1. Henry Lee, *A Funeral Oration in Honor of the Memory of George Washington* (New Haven: Read and Morse, 1800).

2. George Washington to George Mason, April 5, 1769, *The Papers of George Washington, Colonial Series*, vol. 8, *January 1761–June 1767*, edited by W. W. Abbot and Dorothy Twohig (University Press of Virginia, 1993), p. 177–81; Ron Chernow, *Washington: A Life* (New York: Penguin, 2010), p. 145.

3. Washington to Mason, April 5, 1769.

4. David McCullough, *John Adams* (New York: Simon and Schuster, 2001), p. 81.

5. John Adams to Benjamin Rush, August 28, 1811, in *The Works of John Adams: Second President of the United States*, edited by Charles Francis Adams, vol. 2, *Diary, Notes of Debates, Autobiography* (Boston: Little, Brown, 1850), p. 635.

6. McCullough, *John Adams*, pp. 84–85.

7. John Adams to Abigail [Adams], October 9, 1774, in *The Adams Papers, Adams Family Correspondence*, vol. 1, *December 1761–May 1776*, edited by Lyman H. Butterfield (Harvard University Press, 1963), pp. 166–67.

8. Charles-Louis de Secondat, Baron de La Brède et de Montesquieu, *The Spirit of Law*, bk. 20, chap. 1, in *The Complete Works of M. de Montesquieu* (London: T. Evans, 1777).

9. Thomas Jefferson, *Draft of Instructions to the Virginia Delegates in the Continental Congress (MS Text of A Summary View, &c.), [July 1774]* in *The Papers of Thomas Jefferson*, vol. 1, *1760–1776*, edited by Julian P. Boyd (Princeton University Press, 1950), pp. 121–37.

10. George Washington to Robert Mackenzie, October 10, 1774, *The Papers of George Washington, Colonial Series*, vol. 10, *21 March 1774–15 June 1775*, edited by W. W. Abbot and Dorothy Twohig (University Press of Virginia, 1995), pp. 171–72.

11. Lord Dartmouth to General Gage, January 27, 1775, in George Washington, *The Writings of George Washington*, vol. 3, *Correspondence and miscellaneous papers relating to the American Revolution*, edited by Jared Sparks (Boston: American Stationers, John B. Russell, 1834), pt. 2, p. 507.

12. Rick Atkinson, *The British Are Coming: The War for America, Lexington to Princeton, 1775–1777* (New York: Henry Holt, 2019), pp. 53–54.

13. Atkinson, *The British Are Coming*, p. 77.

14. Chernow, *Washington*, p. 187.

15. George Washington, *Address to the New York Provincial Congress, 26 June 1775*, in *The Papers of George Washington, Revolutionary War Series*, vol. 1, *16 June 1775–15 September 1775*, edited by Philander D. Chase (University Press of Virginia, 1985), pp. 41–42. See also Chernow, *Washington*, p. 193: "[Washington] minted a beautiful phrase that must have resonated deeply among his listeners: 'When we assumed the soldier, we did not lay aside the citizen.' The citizen-soldier passed this first test of his political skills with flying colors. Given with perfect pitch, he knew how to talk the language of peace even as he girded for war."

16. Atkinson, *The British Are Coming*, p. 26.

17. George Washington to William Shippen Jr., 6 February 1777, *The Papers of George Washington, Revolutionary War Series*, vol. 8, *January 6, 1777–March 27, 1777*, edited by Frank E. Grizzard Jr. (Charlottesville: University Press of Virginia, 1998), p. 264.

18. Fintan O'Toole, "Vector in Chief," *New York Review of Books*, May 14, 2020; Mary V. Thompson, "Smallpox," George Washington's Mount Vernon.

19. Thomas Jefferson to William Small, 7 May 1775, in *The Papers of Thomas Jefferson*, vol. 1, pp. 165–67.

20. Gillian Hull, "William Small, 1734–1775: No Publications, Much Influence," *Journal of the Royal Society of Medicine* 90 (February 1997), pp. 102–05.

21. Thomas Jefferson to John Randolph, August 25, 1775, *The Papers of Thomas Jefferson*, vol. 1, pp. 240–43.

Chapter 7

Epigraph: Comment upon reading the Declaration of Independence, reported by Benjamin West, an American artist painting the king's portrait. Lewis Einstein, *Divided Loyalties: Americans in England during the War of Independence* (London: Cobden-Sanderson, 1933), p. 307.

1. John Adams, Memorandum of Measures to Be Pursued in Congress, February 1776, in *The Adams Papers, Diary and Autobiography of John Adams*, vol. 2, *1771–1781*, edited by L. H. Butterfield (Harvard University Press, 1961), pp. 229–34. See also David McCullough, *John Adams* (New York: Simon and Schuster, 2001), p. 89. The diary entries are undated. McCullough finds evidence that Adams made the list on route, rather than in Philadelphia.

2. Rick Atkinson, *The British Are Coming: The War for America, Lexington to Princeton, 1775–1777* (New York: Henry Holt, 2019), p. 348.

3. In Adams's telling decades later, he and Jefferson played Alphonse and Gaston. Jefferson suggested that Adams compose the document; Adams demurred and insisted that Jefferson take on the project, arguing,

"Reason first – You are a Virginian, and a Virginian ought to appear at the head of this business. Reason second – I am obnoxious, suspected, and unpopular. You are very much otherwise. Reason third –You can write ten times better than I can." Jefferson recalled no such colloquy. John Adams to Timothy Pickering, August 6, 1822, in *The Works of John Adams, Second President of the United States*, edited by Charles Francis Adams, vol. 2, *Diary, Notes of Debates, and Autobiography* (Boston: Little, Brown, 1856), p. 514.

4. Thomas Jefferson to Henry Lee, May 8, 1825, Monticello, in *The Writings of Thomas Jefferson*, vols. 15–16, edited by Albert Ellery Bergh (Thomas Jefferson Memorial Association of the United States, 1907), pp. 117–18.

5. John Locke, *Two Treatises of Government*; Walter Isaacson, *Benjamin Franklin: An American Life* (New York: Simon and Schuster, 2003), p. 311.

6. Jefferson was not alone in this benign plagiarism. His fellow Virginian and friend, George Mason, used language strikingly similar to Locke's and Jefferson's when drafting the Declaration of Rights of Virginia that was unanimously adopted June 12, 1776, three weeks before the Declaration of Independence: "That all men are by nature equally free and independent and have certain inherent rights, of which, when they enter into a state of society, they cannot, by any compact, deprive or divest their posterity; namely, the enjoyment of life and liberty, with the means of acquiring and possessing property, and pursuing and obtaining happiness and safety." George Mason, *The Best of the OLL No. 45 [George Mason], "The Virginia Bill of Rights" (June, 1776)* (Indianapolis: Liberty Fund, 2013).

7. Declaration of Independence, Records of the Continental and Confederation Congresses and the Constitutional Convention, 1765–1821, National Archives (www.archives.gov/founding-docs/declaration-transcript).

8. Joseph J. Ellis, *American Sphinx: The Character of Thomas Jefferson* (New York: Alfred A. Knopf, 1998), pp. 63–68. See also Joseph J. Ellis, *American Creation: Triumphs and Tragedies at the Founding of the Republic* (New York: Alfred A. Knopf, 2007), p. 56.

9. Danielle Allen, *Our Declaration: A Reading of the Declaration of Independence in Defense of Equality* (New York: Liveright, 2014), p. 136.

10. See Rebecca Newberger Goldstein, *Betraying Spinoza: The Renegade Jew Who Gave Us Modernity* (New York: Schoken Books, 2006), pp. 260–61; Rebecca Newberger Goldstein, "Reasonable Doubt," *New York Times*, July 29, 2006.

11. Author's correspondence with Endrina Tay, associate foundation librarian for technical services, Thomas Jefferson Library, Monticello, Charlottesville, Virginia.

12. Thomas Jefferson to John Adams, April 11, 1823, Monticello, in *The Writings of Thomas Jefferson*, vol. 15–16, edited by Albert Ellery Bergh (Thomas Jefferson Memorial Association of the United States, 1907), pp. 425–30: "Now one sixth of mankind only are supposed to be Christians: the other five sixths then, who do not believe in the Jewish and Christian revelation, are without a knowledge of the existence of a god! This gives compleatly a gain de cause to the disciples of Ocellus, Timaeus, Spinosa, Diderot and D'Holbach."

13. Thomas Jefferson's "original Rough draught" of the Declaration of Independence, in *The Papers of Thomas Jefferson*, vol. 1, *1760–1776*, edited by Julian P. Boyd (Princeton University Press, 1950), pp. 243–47. See Locke's formulations in *Second Treatise on Government*, bk. 2, chap. 2, sec. 6: "Being all equal and independent, no one ought to harm another in his life, health, liberty, or possessions"; and Locke, *An Essay concerning Human Understanding*, bk. 1, chap. 3, sec. 3: "Something of a practical kind that is innate in all mankind, and influences all our conduct, is a desire for happiness and an aversion to misery."

14. Isaacson, *Benjamin Franklin*, p. 312.

15. Danielle Allen argues that the transcript version of the Declaration posted on the National Archives website has a typographical error: the clauses "Life, liberty and the pursuit of Happiness" and "That to secure these rights" are separated by a period. In all drafts copied out by Jefferson and Adams, however, "each of the truths is separated equally from the others with the same punctuation mark," usually a comma. The period

"interrupts an argument that leads from a recognition that individually we all pursue happiness to a subsequent recognition that our best instrument for doing that is what we make together: our government." She makes the case that the change in punctuation disconnects the two clauses—that is, the protection of citizens' rights are organically "secure[d]" by the principle of "the consent of the governed." *Our Declaration*, pp. 278–81.

16. Ellis, *American Sphinx*, pp. 69–70.

17. Jefferson replaced "property," from Locke's formulation, with "happiness." Some scholars have conjectured that *property* would be read as an oblique reference to the issue of slavery.

18. Abigail Adams to John, March 31, 1776, *The Adams Papers, Adams Family Correspondence*, vol. 1, *December 1761–May 1776*, edited by Lyman H. Butterfield (Harvard University Press, 1963), pp. 369–71.

19. John Adams to Abigail, April 14, 1776, *The Adams Papers, Adams Family Correspondence*, vol. 1, pp. 381–83.

20. Eleven years later, Abigail, despairing of progress, fired off a letter to a niece who would be more open to her views:

> Surely as rational Beings, our reason might with propriety receive the highest possible cultivation. Knowledge would teach our Sex candour, and those who aim at the attainment of it, in order to render themselves more amiable & usefull in the world would derive a double advantage from it, for in proportion as the mind is informed, the countanance would be improved & the face ennobled as the Heart is elevated, for wisdom says Soloman maketh the face to shine. Even the Luxurious Eastern Sage thought not of rouge or the milk of roses—but that the virtuous wife should open her mouth with wisdom & the law of kindness dwell upon her Tongue, nor did he think this inconsistant with looking well to the ways of her household, or suppose that she would be less inclined to superintend the domestick oeconomy of her family, for having gone beyond the limits of her dressing room & her kitchen.

Abigail Adams to Lucy Cranch, April 26, 1787, *The Adams Papers, Adams Family Correspondence*, vol. 8, *March 1787–December 1789*, edited by C. James Taylor and others (Harvard University Press, 2007), pp. 24–27. In due course, John came to a truce with Abigail, conceding that her views made intellectual sense. Joseph J. Ellis, *First Family* (New York: Alfred A. Knopf, 2011), p. 51.

21. Benjamin Rush, *An Address to the Inhabitants of the British Settlements, on the Slavery of the Negroes in America*, 2nd ed. (Philadelphia: John Dunlap 1773), p. 30. On Samuel Johnson, see *Taxation No Tyranny: An Answer to the Resolutions and Address of the American Colonies* (London, 1775), 89; also see Peter A. Dorsey, *Common Bondage: Slavery as Metaphor in Revolutionary America* (University of Tennessee Press, 2009), p. 105.

22. Jefferson's "original Rough draught" of the Declaration of Independence, in *The Papers of Thomas Jefferson*.

23. Lucia Stanton, *"Those Who Labor for My Happiness": Slavery at Thomas Jefferson's Monticello* (University of Virginia Press, 2012), p. 106.

24. Ellis, *American Sphinx*, pp. 60–61.

25. Benjamin Rush, *An Address to the Inhabitants of the British Settlements, on the Slavery of the Negroes in America*, 2nd ed. (Philadelphia: John Dunlap 1773), p. 30. On Samuel Johnson, see *Taxation No Tyranny: An Answer to the Resolutions and Address of the American Colonies* (London, 1775), 89; also see Peter A. Dorsey, *Common Bondage: Slavery as Metaphor in Revolutionary America* (University of Tennessee Press, 2009), p. 105.

Chapter 8

Epigraph: Delmore Schwartz, "The Greatest Thing in North America," in *Last & Lost Poems*, edited by Robert S. Phillips (New York: New Directions, 1989), p. 21.

1. Benjamin Rush to John Adams, July 20, 1811, *Letters of Benjamin Rush*, vol. 2, edited by Lyman Henry Butterfield (Princeton University Press, 1951), p. 1090.

Do you recollect your memorable speech upon the Day on which the vote was taken? Do you recollect the pensive and awful silence which pervaded the house when we were called up, one after another, to the table of the President of Congress, to subscribe what was believed by many at that time to be our own death warrants? The silence and the gloom of the morning were interrupted I well recollect, only for a moment by Colonel Harrison of Virginia, who said to Mr. Gerry at the table: "I shall have a great advantage over you, Mr. Gerry, when we are all hung for what we are now doing. From the size and weight of my body I shall die in a few minutes, but from the lightness of your body you will dance in the air an hour or two before you are dead." This speech procured a transient smile, but it was soon succeeded by the solemnity with which the whole business was conducted.

2. George Washington from John Hancock, 6 July 1776, *The Papers of George Washington, Revolutionary War Series*, vol. 5, *16 June 1776–12 August 1776*, edited by Philander D. Chase (University Press of Virginia, 1993), pp. 219–21.

3. Benjamin Franklin to George Washington, June 21, 1776, *The Papers of Benjamin Franklin*, vol. 22, *March 23 1775, through October 27, 1776*, edited by William Wilcox (New Haven and London: Yale University Press, 1982), pp. 484–85.

4. Garry Wills, *Inventing America: Jefferson's Declaration of Independence* (New York: Knopf Doubleday Publishing Group, 2017), p. 318. Frances Hutcheson, *A Short Introduction to Moral Philosophy, in Three Books* (Glasgow, 1747).

5. David Armitage, "The Declaration of Independence: The Words Heard Around the World," *Wall Street Journal*, July 5–6, 2014, p. C1–12.

6. John Adams to T. Digges, May 13, 1780, in *The Works of John Adams, Second President of the United States*, edited by Charles Francis Adams, vol. 7, *Letters and State Papers, 1777–1787* (Boston: Little Brown, 1856), pp. 167–68.

7. Robert Kagan, *Dangerous Nation: America's Place in the World from Its Earliest Days to the Dawn of the 20th Century* (New York: Alfred A. Knopf, 2006), p. 48.

8. Stacy Schiff, *A Great Improvisation: Franklin, France, and the Birth of America* (New York: Henry Holt, 2006), p. 85.

9. Voltaire, "The Works of M. de Voltaire: Additions to the essay on general history. v. 32–33. Miscellaneous poems," vol. 30 of *The Works of M. de Voltaire*, edited by Tobias George Smollett (London: J. Newbery, R. Baldwin, W. Johnston, S. Crowder, T. Davies, J. Coote, G. Kerasley, and B. Collins, 1763), p. 156.

10. Schiff, *A Great Improvisation*, pp. 14–15.

11. Jean-Jacques Rousseau, *The Social Contract*, bk. 1, chap. 1, translated by Rose M. Harrington (London: G. P. Putnam's Sons, 1893), p. 2.

12. This quote is commonly attributed to Diderot, although he may have borrowed the language from a French atheist priest, Jean Meslier (1664–1729). The phrase appears in Meslier's memoir, which was published posthumously by Voltaire, another copycat of Meslier's. Jean Meslier, *Testament: Memoir of the Thoughts and Sentiments of Jean Meslier*, translated by Michael Shreve (Amherst, Mass.: Prometheus Books, 2009), p. 37.

13. Niall Ferguson, *Empire: The Rise and Demise of the British World Order and the Lessons for Global Power* (New York: Basic Books, 2004), p. 29.

14. Schiff, *A Great Improvisation*, p. 123.

15. The American Commissioners to the Committee of Secret Correspondence, 12 March [–9 April 1777], in *The Papers of Benjamin Franklin*, vol. 23, *October 27, 1776, through April 30, 1777*, edited by William B. Willcox (Yale University Press, 1983), pp. 466–76. It was signed by Franklin and Silas Deane, a subordinate official who arrived in Paris before Franklin. Before becoming a diplomat, Deane was a delegate to the Continental Congress; later, he was charged with financial improprieties and accused of deeming the cause of independence hopeless. He lived in Europe and died under mysterious circumstances while trying to return to the United States.

16. Benjamin Franklin to Samuel Cooper, 1 May 1777, *The Papers of Benjamin Franklin*, vol. 24, *May 1 through September 30, 1777*, edited by William B. Willcox (Yale University Press, 1984), pp. 6–7.

17. Benjamin Franklin, *The Compleated Autobiography*, edited by Mark Skousen (Washington, D.C.: Regnery Publishing, 2006), p. 145.

18. Jean-Antoine-Nicolas de Caritat, Marquis of Condorcet, Eulogy of Benjamin Franklin, read at the public session of the Academy of Sciences, November 13, 1790, in *Condorcet: Writings on the United States*, edited by Guillaume Ansart (Pennsylvania State University Press, 2012), p. 105.

19. Cited in Walter Isaacson, *Benjamin Franklin: An American Life* (New York: Simon and Schuster, 2003), p. 339.

20. Isaacson, *Benjamin Franklin*, p. 342.

21. "The American Commissioners to [the Comte de Vergennes], 4 December 1777," in *The Papers of Benjamin Franklin*, vol. 25, *October 1, 1777, through February 28, 1778*, edited by William B. Willcox (Yale University Press, 1986), pp. 236–37.

22. Ron Chernow, *Washington: A Life* (New York: Penguin, 2010), p. 315.

23. Paul Wentworth to [William Eden]: Extract, 7 January 1778, in *The Papers of Benjamin Franklin*, vol. 25, pp. 435–40.

24. Wentworth to [William Eden]: Extract.

25. James Parton, *Life and Times of Benjamin Franklin*, vol. 2 (New York: Mason Brothers Publishing, 1865), p. 294; Isaacson, *Benjamin Franklin*, pp. 416–17.

26. Chernow, *Washington*, p. 335.

27. Edmund Morgan, *The Birth of the Republic: 1763–1789* (University of Chicago Press, 1956), pp. 82–83.

28. Chernow, *Washington*, p. 418. Lin-Manuel Miranda alludes to the phrase in the original song "Yorktown" in his 2015 Broadway musical *Hamilton*, which was based loosely on Chernow's biography of Alexander Hamilton.

29. Chernow, *Washington*, p. 457.

30. "Charles E. Stanton, 'Lafayette, We Are Here'" (1917), in *Speeches in World History*, by Suzanne McIntire (New York: Infobase Publishing, 2009), p. 307.

31. *Circular to the States: George Washington to the States*, 8 June 1783, transcript, George Washington's Mount Vernon.

32. Garry Wills, *Cincinnatus: George Washington and the Enlightenment* (Garden City, N.Y.: Doubleday, 1984), p. 13.

33. Isaacson, *Benjamin Franklin*, pp. 353–56.

34. John Adams to John Quincy Adams, 11 August 1777, *The Adams Papers, Adams Family Correspondence*, vol. 2, *June 1776–March 1778*, edited by L. H. Butterfield (Harvard University Press, 1963), pp. 307–08.

35. John Adams, *The Works of John Adams, Second President of the United States*, edited by Charles Francis Adams, vol. 3, *Autobiography, Diary, Notes of a Debate, in the Senate, Essays* (Boston: Little, Brown, 1856), diary entry for February 11, 1779; Joseph J. Ellis, *Passionate Sage: The Character and Legacy of John Adams* (New York: W. W. Norton, 1993), pp. 11–12.

36. John Adams to William Temple Franklin, 7 December 1780, in *The Adams Papers, Papers of John Adams*, vol. 10, *July 1780–December 1780*, edited by Gregg L. Lint and Richard Alan Ryerson (Harvard University Press, 1996), p. 398; John E. Ferling, *John Adams: A Life* (Oxford University Press, 1992), pp. 228–30.

37. Joan Derk van der Capellen tot den Pol to John Adams: A Translation, 28 November 1780, in *The Adams Papers, Papers of John Adams*, vol. 10, pp. 378–81. See also David McCullough, *John Adams* (New York: Simon and Schuster, 2001), p. 255.

38. McCullough, *John Adams*, pp. 268–69.

39. John Adams to Francis Dana, 18 April 1781, *The Adams Papers, Papers of John Adams*, vol. 11, *January–September 1781*, edited by Gregg L. Lint and others (Harvard University Press, 2003), pp. 267–70.

40. William V was a descendent of William III of England, who made possible Locke's return home in the previous century. For the genealogy, see the House of Orange family tree at https://en.wikipedia.org/wiki/Family_tree_of_the_House_of_Orange_(1450%E2%80%931815).

41. McCullough, *John Adams*, pp. 270–71.

42. John Adams to Abigail Adams, 1 July 1782, *The Adams Papers, Adams Family Correspondence*, vol. 4, *October 1780–September 1782*, edited by L. H. Butterfield and Marc Friedlaender (Harvard University Press, 1973), pp. 337–39.

Chapter 9

Epigraph: *Federalist* No. 1

1. The Paris Peace Treaty of September 30, 1783, in *Treaties and Other International Acts of the United States of America*, vol. 2, "Documents 1-40: 1776–1818," edited by David Hunter Miller (Washington: Government Printing Office, 1931).

2. John Adams to John Jay, 2 June 1785, *The Adams Papers, Papers of John Adams*, vol. 17, *April–November 1785*, edited by Gregg L. Lint and others (Harvard University Press, 2014), pp. 134–45. See also Stanley Ayling, *George the Third* (New York: Alfred A. Knopf, 1972), p. 323.

3. John Adams, *The Works of John Adams, Second President of the United States*, edited by Charles Francis Adams, vol. 8, *Letters and State Papers, 1782–1799* (Boston: Little, Brown, 1856), p. 257. See also David McCullough, *John Adams* (New York: Simon and Schuster, 2001), pp. 335–36.

4. Bill Providing for Delegates to the Convention of 1787 [6 November], in *The Papers of James Madison*, vol. 9, *9 April 1786–24 May 1787 and supplement 1781–1784*, edited by Robert A. Rutland and William M. E. Rachal (University of Chicago Press, 1975), pp. 163–64.

5. George Washington to Alexander Hamilton, *The Papers of Alexander Hamilton*, vol. 3, *1782–1786*, edited by Harold C. Syrett (Columbia University Press, 1962), pp. 309–11.

6. George Washington to James Warren, 7 October 1785, *The Papers of George Washington, Confederation Series*, vol. 3, *19 May 1785–31 March 1786*, edited by W. W. Abbot (University Press of Virginia, 1994), pp. 298–301.

7. George Washington to James Madison, 30 November 1785, *The Papers of George Washington, Confederation Series*, vol. 3, pp. 419–42.

8. "Benjamin Franklin: Speech in Convention, 17 September 1787," *The Documentary History of the Ratification of the Constitution Digital Edition*, edited by John P. Kaminski and others (University of Virginia Press, 2009). See also Walter Isaacson, *Benjamin Franklin: An American Life* (Yale University Press, 2005), pp. 457–59.

9. James McHenry, *Diary, September 18, 1787*, manuscript, James

McHenry Papers, Manuscript Division, Library of Congress (63.02.00). Scholars are uncertain whether the lady in question was Powel. When she was asked in 1814, she did not remember the exchange, but she wrote in a letter, "I have no recollection of any such conversations. . . . Yet I cannot venture to deny after so many Years have elapsed that such conversations had passed." Elizabeth Willing Powel to Martha Hare, April 25, 1814, *Powel Family Papers*, Historical Society of Pennsylvania. In any case, Franklin's seven-word retort to the question has reverberated for more than two centuries, especially in the Age of Trump.

10. Joseph J. Ellis, *The Quartet: Orchestrating the Second American Revolution, 1783–1789* (New York: Vintage, 2016), p. 126.

11. David Hume, *An Enquiry Concerning the Principles of Morals* (London: A. Millar, 1751), p. 100.

12. "The Federalist Number 10, [22 November] 1787," in *The Papers of James Madison*, vol. 10, *27 May 1787–3 March 1788*, edited by Robert A. Rutland and others (University of Chicago Press, 1977), pp. 263–70.

13. "The Federalist No. 1, [27 October 1787]," in *The Papers of Alexander Hamilton*, vol. 4, *January 1787–May 1788*, edited by Harold C. Syrett (Columbia University Press, 1962), pp. 301–06.

14. Alexander Hamilton, "Enclosure: [Objections and Answers Respecting the Administration], [18 August 1792]," in *The Papers of Alexander Hamilton*, vol. 12, *July 1792–October 1792*, edited by Harold C. Syrett (Columbia University Press, 1967), pp. 229–58.

Chapter 10

Epigraph: To George Washington from Alexander Hamilton, 13 August 1788, *The Papers of George Washington, Confederation Series*, vol. 6, *1 January 1788–23 September 1788*, edited by W. W. Abbot (Charlottesville: University Press of Virginia, 1997), pp. 443–44.

1. Garry Wills, *Cincinnatus: George Washington and the Enlightenment* (Garden City, N.Y.: Doubleday, 1984), p. 23.

2. Joseph Ellis, *His Excellency: George Washington* (New York: Alfred A. Knopf, 2004), pp. 188–89.

3. James David Barber, *The Presidential Character: Predicting Perfor-

mance in the White House (Englewood Cliffs, N.J.: Prentice-Hall, 1972), p. 4.

4. George Washington to Charles Cotesworth Pinckney, 22 January 1794, *The Papers of George Washington, Presidential Series*, vol. 15, *January 1–30 April 1794*, edited by Christine Sternberg Patrick (University of Virginia Press, 2009), pp. 103–05.

5. In his farewell address in 1796, Washington declared a similar conviction: "It is substantially true that virtue or morality is a necessary spring of popular government." *The Papers of George Washington*, vol. 20, *1 April–21 September 1796*, edited by David R. Hoth and William M. Ferraro (University of Virginia Press, 2019).

6. George Washington to James Madison, 5 May 1789, *The Papers of George Washington, Presidential Series*, vol. 2, *1 April 1789–15 June 1789*, edited by Dorothy Twohig (University Press of Virginia, 1987), pp. 216–17.

7. George Washington to John Adams, 10 May 1789, *Papers of George Washington, Presidential Series*, vol. 2, pp. 245–50.

8. In 2018 there was a flurry of news reports that Washington might not have returned the books. See Corey Kilgannon, "President Washington, Your Library Books Are Overdue," *New York Times*, June 13, 2018. The library has posted its own interpretation on its website: see Matthew Bright, "The Curious Case of the President's Overdue Books," February 17, 2017. In any case, no fines were issued.

9. George Washington to Catherine Sawbridge Macaulay Graham, January 9, 1790, *The Papers of George Washington, Presidential Series*, vol. 4, *8 September 1789–15 January 1790*, edited by Dorothy Twohig (Charlottesville: University Press of Virginia, 1993), pp. 551–54; Joseph Ellis, *His Excellency: George Washington* (New York: Alfred A. Knopf, 2004), p. 189.

10. Joseph J. Ellis, *Founding Brothers: The Revolutionary Generation* (New York: Random House: Vintage Books, 2000), p. 47.

11. Ron Chernow, *Alexander Hamilton* (New York: Penguin Press, 2004), p. 405.

12. Ellis, *Founding Brothers*, p. 223.

13. Jefferson to Adams, October 28, 1813, *The Papers of Thomas Jefferson*, Retirement Series, vol. 6, *11 March to 27 November 1813*, edited by J. Jefferson Looney (Princeton: Princeton University Press, 2009), pp. 562–68.

Index